DAVID WENTZ

John Wesley's Christian Perfection

*Set in Modern Language with Introduction and
Suggestions for Group Use*

DOING CHRISTIANITY
Pastor David Wentz

Contents

Introduction

"Christians aren't perfect, just forgiven." Surely a claim that shows up on so many bumper stickers, T-shirts, and coffee mugs must be true, right?

John Wesley, founder of Methodism and grandfather of Pentecostalism and the Salvation Army, would beg to differ. In fact, Wesley taught that every Christian who has grown past spiritual infancy is far more than just forgiven, they are actually perfect.

"But that's nuts!" probably 99% of readers say at this point. "Nobody's perfect!"

That's exactly the response probably 99% of Wesley's listeners had in 1741, when "Christian Perfection," sermon #40 in Wesley's Standard Sermons, was first published.

For a hundred and fifty years Methodists were laughed at, and sometimes persecuted, even as their numbers grew exponentially. Much of the derision was aimed at their distinctive doctrine of Christian perfection. Many believe it's more than a coincidence that as the emphasis on perfection waned, both the laughter and the growth plateaued and then began to decline.

This book is not intended to show you how to revitalize your church by preaching perfection, although that might be an interesting experiment. Our goal here is to look at what caused all the excitement in the first place.

Words Matter

In many ways the whole upheaval about Christian perfection might have been avoided if King James' translators had chosen a different word. The New Testament was originally written in Greek. The Greek word translated "perfect" is *telios*. As often happens when translating from one language to another, shades of meaning can be missed.

For instance, most Americans think of the Hawaiian word *aloha* as meaning "hello" or "goodbye." While it is used in those senses, the full meaning is not, "I'm here" or "I'm leaving," but something along the lines of, "I greet (or leave) you with wishes of love, peace, and respect."

In the same way, while "perfect" is a good translation of *telios*, it doesn't convey all the nuances. At its root, *telios* means completeness, maturity, and having attained a goal. The English word "perfect," on the other hand, usually implies flawless, without a blemish, and without mistake. So while "perfect" may be the best one-word translation of *telios*, it misses some important shades of meaning, and suggests others that don't apply.

John Wesley certainly knew all this; after all, he taught Greek and New Testament at Oxford University. So why didn't he use a different word and avoid all the controversy? Because "perfect" is the word his hearers saw in their Bibles. As a pastor, Wesley had one goal for his preaching: to make the Bible as clear as possible to his people and to equip and motivate them to follow it, by the grace of the Holy Spirit. He wrote, "I design plain truth for plain people . . . I labor to avoid all words which are not easy to be understood, all which are not used in common life."[1]

Words Change

Wesley's logic, clarity, and Biblical truth are as potent today as they ever were. Unfortunately, his eighteenth-century English is more and more difficult for modern readers to understand. Wesley was a revival preacher with the best of them; people were often so struck by his words that they cried out and even fell to the ground.

Today, the mental effort of interpreting his sometimes archaic phrases can rob them of their power.

That's where this book comes in. It updates Wesley's English to be clear to the modern reader while maintaining his distinctive writing and preaching style. My goal is not only to help you understand Wesley's points but to give a sense of what it was like to hear him preach. For scholars and the curious, Wesley's original is included as an appendix.

John's younger brother Charles was an integral partner in the Methodist movement. John was the preacher and Charles was the songwriter (though Charles often preached and John wrote a few songs). John's sermons and Charles' hymns taught the same message in different ways. That's why printed versions of John's "Christian Perfection" sermon were often accompanied by the words to Charles' hymn, "The Promise of Sanctification." All twenty-four verses are included in Appendix 2. You can sing it to the tune of "Amazing Grace."

Wesley's Method for Finding Spiritual Truth

In the preface to the first collection of sermons John Wesley published, he explained his method for finding spiritual truth:[2]

To candid, reasonable people I am not afraid to lay open what have been the inmost thoughts of my heart. I have thought, *I am a creature of the day, passing through life, as an arrow through the air. I am a spirit come from God, and returning to God: just hovering over the great gulf; till a few moments from now, I am no more seen! I drop into an unchangeable eternity! I want to know one thing, the way to heaven: how to land safe on that happy shore.*

God himself has condescended to teach the way. For this very reason he came from heaven. He has written it down in a book! Oh give me that book! At any price, give me the book of God!

I have it! Here is knowledge enough for me. Let me be a man of one book.

Here I am then, far from the busy ways of people. I sit down alone. Only God is here. And in his presence I open and read this book. My purpose: to find the way to heaven.

Is there a doubt concerning the meaning of something I read? Does anything appear unclear or confusing?

I lift up my heart to the Father of lights, praying: *Lord, doesn't your word say, If anyone lacks wisdom, let him ask of God? You give generously and ungrudgingly.*[3] *You said if anyone is willing to do your will, they shall know.*[4] *I am willing! Let me know your will.*

Then I search after and consider parallel passages of scripture, comparing spiritual things with spiritual.[5]

I meditate on it,[6] with all the attention and earnestness of which my mind is capable.

4

If any doubt still remains, I consult those who are experienced in the things of God, and the writings of those who have gone before.

And what I learn in this way, that is what I teach.

Wesley's Method of Teaching

One of the main things Wesley felt he learned from the Bible, and therefore felt he had to teach, was Christian perfection. As befitting the founder of what came to be called Methodism, he presents his case very methodically. Many modern pastors do not use this kind of approach, so let's take a moment to examine Wesley's argument style.

Wesley's entire case is based on the premise that the Bible is God's authoritative word to his people. Among other things, this means:

1. Whatever the Bible says is true.
2. If we properly understand what a Bible passage says, we can call that understanding a Bible truth.
3. Like all other truths, Bible truths can be used as the basis for logical reasoning.
4. If the cited Bible truths are properly understood and applied and the logical reasoning is properly done, then the conclusions must be equally true.
5. If Bible truths, or conclusions properly derived from them, contradict human experience or reasoning, then the human experience or reasoning conflicts with truth and must be reinterpreted to match the Bible, not the other way around.

Wesley believed and practiced this so strongly that he even based some of his arguments in this sermon on the particular wording of the verses — just as the apostle Paul did when he based an argument on the fact that "offspring" is singular instead of plural in Galatians 3:16.[7]

Notes on the Paraphrase

John Wesley read and wrote widely on many subjects, including electricity and medicine. Still, he called himself "a man of one book." That book was the Bible. His sermons are liberally sprinkled with Scripture quotations and allusions. Wesley read the Bible in Greek, Hebrew, and probably German, but for him the English Bible was the King James Version (KJV), translated in 1611. For many modern readers, that seventeenth-century English can be even more difficult than Wesley's eighteenth-century phrasing. So for most Bible references in this paraphrase, I chose either the New Revised Standard Version (NRSV) or the New King James Version (NKJV). Both are clear, accurate translations that trace their literary lineage back to the KJV Wesley used. The NRSV is more widely used in Methodist churches, so that was my first choice. In some cases, where the New King James more closely reflected Wesley's wording, I used that translation, with the notation NKJV. In some cases Wesley's argument hinges on the particular wording of the King James Version. In those places I quoted the words Wesley was quoting. For clarity, verses and phrases that are direct quotes from the Bible are placed in italics. The many places where Wesley alluded to Scripture without specifically quoting it are in regular print. All quotes and allusions are end-noted.

The methodical Wesley commonly used the technique of numbering his paragraphs. I have replaced the numbers with subheadings and divided his long block paragraphs into shorter ones to reflect modern usage.

"He Can't Be Serious!"

As a result of Wesley's approach, as you go through his sermon you're likely to come across some statements that strike you as unrealistic, if not downright radical. I can make the language easier for our minds to understand, but I can't make his assertions easier for our human nature to accept. But isn't the same true of many things Jesus said?

Wesley just took difficult Bible passages, clearly explained them, and carried them to their logical conclusion — without the exceptions and excuses we so often like to add. The result describes a whole new way of living.

What would it look like if we were to rediscover this Wesleyan ideal? What would it look like if every local church in every denomination that traces its heritage back to Wesley were to become known as a place where people are actively trying to live the way Wesley describes, not stopping at salvation but moving on toward a new life that perfectly reflects the nature of Jesus?

Frankly, we might lose some members at first, because Wesley's Methodism is not an easy feel-good religion. But if people today are anything like they were when Wesley preached – and I believe they are, because human nature doesn't change – a lot of people would find this type of Christianity immensely attractive.

"Nobody's perfect." John Wesley would say that's a cop-out. With God's help everyone can be perfect, and should be.

Suggestions for Group Use

John Wesley wrote *Christian Perfection* as a sermon, and there is power in reading it straight through in that way. However, as with all thought-provoking books, Wesley's words will have the greatest impact on our individual lives and on our churches when we think them through with others.

That was part of Wesley's method. He organized his followers into small groups called classes which met weekly, usually in people's homes. Their main purpose was to discuss how they could be better Christians, based on the previous week's sermon, and to hold each other accountable for acting that way. As they met, they experienced a joyful fellowship. In the modern phrase, they were "doing life together."

This book is perfectly suited for that kind of small-group experience. It can be a home group, a coffee shop gathering, or an adult Sunday School class. To facilitate such use, I've broken the material into six parts. Each should take less than fifteen minutes to read. I've also included some suggested discussion questions at the end of each part, to get you started.

How to Lead a Small Group

Small group gatherings are easy. You can meet in the same place every time, or in different people's homes. You can have the same leader every time, or rotate leadership. (Being the leader isn't a big deal. The leader is just the person who reads the discussion questions out loud.) A good time frame is an hour to an hour and a half. The tried and true format goes something like this:

- People arrive, say hello, and perhaps munch on some light refreshments.
- Somebody says a prayer to get things started, asking God to guide the conversation and bless anyone who is missing.
- You catch up on anything left over from last week – especially including any good stories about how the study helped someone during the week.
- You talk about as many of the discussion questions as you have time for. Answer the ones that interest you, or make up your own.
- You set the place, time, and assignments for the next meeting.
- You share prayer concerns and pray for them.
- You go out and live what you've been talking about.

If anyone was absent, the leader or a designated person should call them within a day. Tell them you missed them, see if anything is wrong, and catch them up on what happened. Don't forget to tell them the details of the next meeting.

Suggested Schedule

Six weeks is a good, non-threatening length of time for most people to commit to a study like this. Here is a suggested six-week schedule.

Week 1: Introduction

Week 2: Perfect? Us?

Week 3: Real Christians Don't Sin

Week 4: "But Doesn't the Bible Say?" Old Testament

Week 5: "But Doesn't the Bible Say?" New Testament

Week 6: Free Inside

* * *

Discussion Questions

(1) What is your church background?

a. A denomination or tradition that traces back to John Wesley

b. Another Christian denomination or tradition

c. A Christian church but not sure of the roots

d. A variety of different churches

e. Not raised as a church-goer

(2) Do you believe there is value in knowing the historic roots of your faith tradition? Why or why not?

(3) The introduction cites the popular sayings, "Nobody's perfect," and "Christians aren't perfect, just forgiven." How can those ideas be used as excuses for not striving to become more like Jesus?

(4) Does Wesley's method for finding spiritual truth seem reasonable for modern Christians? Why or why not?

(5) Have you ever heard a sermon that used Wesley's teaching method? Did you find it convincing?

(6) What do you hope to gain from this study?

1

"Christian Perfection," by John Wesley

Perfect? Us?

Not as though I had already attained, either were already perfect. — Philippians 3:12[8]

There is hardly any passage in Holy Scripture which has given more offense than this one. The word "perfect" is what many can't bear. The very sound of it greatly offends them. And whoever "preaches perfection" (as the phrase goes), that is, claims that perfection is attainable in this life, runs great risk of being considered worse than an atheist.

For this reason, some have advised me to completely stop using those phrases, "because they have so greatly offended people." But aren't they found in the Bible? Then by what authority can anyone who speaks for God lay them aside, even if everyone will be offended? This is not how we have learned to follow Christ. We will not give place to the devil in this way. Whatever God has spoken, that is what we will speak, whether people will hear us or not; because we know that the only way any minister of Christ can avoid being responsible for people's eternal death is by unshrinkingly declaring the whole purpose of God.[9]

So we can't lay aside these phrases. They are the words God, not of humans. But we can and ought to explain the meaning of them, so those who are sincere in heart won't get off course, to the right or the left, from the path toward the prize of their high calling.[10]

This explanation is clearly needed, because in our text verse Paul speaks of himself as not yet perfect: *Not*, he says, *as though I were already perfect.*[11] And yet immediately afterward, three verses later, he speaks of himself — yes, and many others — as perfect. *Let us, therefore*, he says, *as many as be perfect, be thus minded.*[12]

I'd like to remove any difficulty arising from this seeming contradiction. I'd also like to give light to those who are pressing forward toward the mark of Christian growth, and help those who are struggling so they can stay on the right path.

To do this, I want to show two things: first, in what sense Christians are not perfect; and second, in what sense they are.

First, I'll show in what sense Christians are not perfect. Both from experience and Scripture, several facts are apparent.

Christians Are Not Perfect in Knowledge

First, Christians are not perfect in knowledge. They are not so perfect in this life as to be free from ignorance.

Like everyone, they may know many things about the present world, and they know the general truths God has revealed about the world to come.

13

Christians also know some things that people of the world do not receive, because they are only understood spiritually.[13]

They know *what love the Father has given us, that we should be called children of God.*[14]

They know the mighty working of God's Spirit in their hearts.[15]

They know the wisdom of God's providence, directing all their paths[16] and causing all things to work together for their good.[17]

They know, in every circumstance of life, what the Lord requires of them.[18]

They know how to keep a clear conscience toward God and all people.[19]

But the things Christians do not know are beyond number.

Concerning the Almighty himself, they cannot perfectly understand everything. *These are but the outskirts of his ways . . . the thunder of his power who can understand?*[20] It's not just that they can't understand the most difficult points, like how there are three that bear record in heaven, the Father, the Son, and the Holy Spirit, and these three are one;[21] or how the eternal Son of God took upon himself the form of a servant.[22] They can't even fully understand a single attribute, not one circumstance of the divine nature.

Neither is it for them to know the times and seasons when God will work his great works upon the earth,[23] not even those which he has in part revealed by his servants and prophets since the world began.[24] Much less do they know when God, having fulfilled the number of his elect, will reveal his kingdom, when *the heavens shall pass away with a loud noise and the elements will be dissolved with fire.*[25]

Christians do not even know the reasons for much of what

God does with the human race. They just have to rest in the fact that, even when it seems that *clouds and thick darkness are all around him*, nevertheless *righteousness and justice are the foundation of his throne.*[26] Indeed, often with regard to God's dealings with themselves, their Lord says to them, *You do not know now what I am doing, but later you will understand.*[27]

And how little do Christians know of what is always in front of them, the visible works of God's hands! How *he stretches the north over empty space,* and *hangs the earth on nothing.*[28] How he unites all the parts of this vast cosmic machine by a secret chain that cannot be broken. So great is the ignorance, so very little the knowledge, of even the best people!

No one, then, is so perfect in this life as to be free from ignorance.

Christians Are Not Free From Mistakes

Second, Christians are not perfect in being free from mistakes. Indeed, mistakes are an almost unavoidable consequence of ignorance, seeing that those who *know only in part*[29] are always liable to be wrong about the parts they don't know.

It is true that the children of God do not make mistakes about the things essential to salvation. They don't *put darkness for light and light for darkness;*[30] neither do they "seek death in the error of their life."[31] This is because they are taught by God,[32] and what he teaches them, *the holy way,* is so plain that *no traveler, not even fools, shall go astray.*[33]

But in things not essential to salvation, Christians do make mistakes, and frequently.

The best and wisest of them are frequently mistaken with regard to facts. They believe something is not true when it

15

really is, or something was done that was not. Or if they are not mistaken as to the fact itself, they may be quite wrong about some or all of the circumstances surrounding it; and that can't help but cause more mistakes.

They may believe past or present actions which were or are evil to be good, and those that were or are good to be evil. This may lead them to false judgments about people's character; they might think good people are better than they are, or wicked people are worse. They might even think bad people are good, and holy people beyond reproach are evil.

Even with regard to the Holy Scriptures themselves, as careful as they are to avoid them, the best people are liable to make mistakes. In fact, they do it every day, especially about those parts of the Bible that go beyond simple instructions about how to live. So even the children of God are not agreed as to the interpretation of many places in the Bible. These differences of opinion are not any proof that those on either side are not children of God. But it is proof that we shouldn't expect any living person to be infallible, any more than we expect them to be all-knowing.

Someone might object to all this by quoting the apostle John, where he wrote to his brothers and sisters in the faith, *You have an anointing from the Holy One, and you know all things.*[34]

The answer is plain: You know all things that are needful for your souls' health.[35] The apostle never intended to extend this farther, in an absolute sense. This is clear from two observations.

First, if by "you know all things" he meant that Christians have all knowledge, he would be saying that Christian disciples are above their master Jesus, because there were things Christ himself, as a man, didn't know. *But about that day or hour,* he

16

said, *no one knows, neither the angels in heaven, nor the Son, but only the Father.*[36]

Second, it's clear from the apostle's own words that follow, where he says, *I write these things to you concerning those who would deceive you*[37] — as well as his frequently repeated caution, *Let no one deceive you.*[38] This warning would be altogether needless unless those very people who had that *anointing from the Holy One* were liable, not just to ignorance, but to mistakes also.

Christians Are Not Free From Weaknesses

So Christians are not so perfect as to be free either from ignorance or error. We may add a third point: Christians are not free from weaknesses.

Only let's be careful to understand this word properly; let's not give this title to what are actually sins, as some like to do. One person tells us, "Every man has his weakness, and mine is drunkenness." Another has the "weakness" of pornography, another of using God's holy name as a curse word, yet another of calling people names,[39] or returning insult for insult.[40] It is plain that all you who talk like this, if you don't repent, shall, with your "weaknesses," go quickly into hell!

As to the actual weaknesses to which Christians may be subject, I do not limit them to what might properly be called physical weaknesses. I also include all those inward or outward imperfections which are not of a moral nature. These include slowness of understanding, mental dullness or confusion, incoherent thought, unusual highs or lows of imagination, or the lack of a good memory, either in quickly remembering things or retaining memories over time.[41] And I could go on.

Other weaknesses are the result of those just listed: slowness of speech, using wrong words, pronouncing things wrong — we could add a thousand other nameless defects, either in speech or behavior.

All these are found to some extent even in the best people. And no one can hope to be perfectly freed from them until they breathe their last and the spirit returns to God who gave it.[42]

Christians Are Not Free From Temptations

Until that time, as well, we cannot expect to be completely free from temptation.

It's true that many people may seem to be without temptation. There are some who are so greedy to practice every kind of impure thought[43] that they are hardly aware that those thoughts are actually temptations they are failing to resist.

There are also many who have been lulled to spiritual sleep by their faith in the dead husk of religious activities.[44] The clever enemy of souls will not tempt these to major sins, for fear that they may wake up and realize their danger before they drop into everlasting burnings.

I know there are also children of God who, having been freely set right with God[45] and having found redemption in the blood of Christ,[46] for the present feel no temptation. God has said to their enemies, "Do not touch my anointed ones, and do my children no harm."[47] For this season, it may be for weeks or months, he causes them to ride on high places,[48] he bears them up as on eagles' wings[49] above *all the flaming arrows of the evil one.*[50] But this state will not last always, as we may learn from this one fact: that the Son of God himself, in the days of his flesh, was tempted even to the end of his life.[51] Therefore, his servants should expect the same, for it is enough that they be like their master.[52]

* * *

Discussion Questions

(1) How many sermons have you heard about Christian perfection?

a. How well do you think you understand it?

b. Would you like to hear more?

(2) "For this reason, some have advised me to completely stop using those phrases, 'because they have so greatly offended people.' But aren't they found in the Bible? Then by what authority can anyone who speaks for God lay them aside, even if everyone will be offended?" How do you balance quoting the Bible against potentially offending people?

(3)Wesley says Christians are not free from mistakes. What is the funniest mistake you ever heard someone make in church?

(4)Wesley writes of drunkenness, pornography, and other behaviors, "Let's be careful to understand this word [weaknesses] properly; let's not give this title to what are actually sins, as some like to do."

a. Are these moral weaknesses, sicknesses, or sins?

b. What is the difference?

(5) Wesley warns against "faith in the dead husk of religious activities."

a. What religious activities have become "dead husks" to you? How can you make them more alive?

b. What religious activities help you in your faith? Why?

2

Real Christians Don't Sin

Christian perfection, therefore, contrary to what some seem to imagine, does not imply an exemption from ignorance or mistakes or weaknesses or temptations. Instead, it's just another name for holiness. They are two names for the same thing. So everyone who is perfect is holy, and everyone who is holy is, in the Bible sense, perfect.

But we may make one last observation: even in this respect there is no absolute perfection on earth. There is no "perfection of degrees," as it is called; there is always room for improvement. So no matter how much a person has attained, no matter how perfect they have become, there is still a need to *grow in grace*,[53] and daily to advance in the knowledge and love of our Savior God.[54]

Christians Grow in Stages

In what sense, then, are Christians perfect? This is what I shall now endeavor to show.

But first it should be stated that there are several stages in Christian life, as in natural life. Some of the children of God are just new-born babies. Others have attained to more maturity. This is why St. John, in his first epistle, addresses himself separately to those he calls *little children,* those he calls *young men,* and those he calls *fathers.*

I am writing to you, little children, says the apostle, *because your sins are forgiven on account of his name*[55] — because you have gotten this far: being freely set right with God, you have peace with God through Jesus Christ.[56]

I am writing to you, young people, because you have conquered the evil one; or, as he afterward adds, *because you are strong and the word of God abides in you, and you have overcome the evil one.*[57] You have *quenched the flaming arrows of the evil one,*[58] the doubts and fears by which he disturbed your peace at first, and now God's assurance that your sins are forgiven lives in your heart.

I write to you, fathers, because you have known Him who is from the beginning.[59] You have known the Father and the Son and the Spirit of Christ in your inmost soul. You are *perfect,* being grown up to *the measure of the stature of the fullness of Christ.*[60]

These are the people I mainly speak of in the rest of this sermon, because these are the only ones who are properly Christians. But even babies in Christ are perfect, or born of God (an expression also taken in various ways), in the first sense: that they do not commit sin.

Real Christians Don't Sin

If anyone doubts this privilege of the children of God, the question is not to be decided by abstract reasonings, which may be drawn out endlessly and still leave the question just as it was before. Neither is it to be determined by the experience of this or that particular person. Many may suppose they do not sin, when they do; but this proves nothing either way. Our appeal must be to the Bible. *Let God be true but every man a liar.*[61] By his word we will abide, and that alone. This is how we ought to be judged.

Now the word of God plainly declares that even those who are born again in the lowest sense, that of justification or forgiveness,[62] do not continue in sin. They cannot go on living in it.[63] They are united together in the likeness of the death of Christ,[64] so that their old nature is *crucified with him.* This means the *body of sin is destroyed,* so that from now on they do not serve sin;[65] they are dead with Christ and therefore *freed from sin.*[66] They are *dead to sin, and alive to God.*[67] Sin has *no more dominion* over them, because they are now *not under law, but under grace.*[68] Instead, *having been set free from sin,* they *have become slaves of righteousness.*[69]

The very least that can be implied in these words is that the persons they speak of — namely, all real Christians, or believers in Christ — have been made free from outward sin. Paul here has used a variety of phrases to express that same freedom Peter describes in this one: *Whoever has suffered in the flesh has finished with sin, so as to live for the rest of your earthly life no longer by human desires but by the will of God.*[70] "Finished with sin," even if it is interpreted in the lowest sense as regarding only outward behavior, must at least mean ceasing from outward acts of sin or breaking God's law.

John is even clearer in the well-known words of his first epistle. From the third chapter:

Everyone who commits sin is a child of the devil; for the devil has been sinning from the beginning. The Son of God was revealed for this purpose, to destroy the works of the devil. Those who have been born of God do not sin, because God's seed abides in them; they cannot sin, because they have been born of God.[71]

And from the fifth chapter:

We know that those who are born of God do not sin, but the one who was born of God protects them, and the evil one does not touch them.[72]

Some say, "This only means they don't sin willfully, or they don't commit sin habitually, or they aren't as bad as other people, or they're not as bad as they were before." But who says this? St. John? No. There's nothing like that in these verses — or in the whole chapter, or in the whole letter, or in anything he wrote at all!

The best way to answer this kind of bald assertion is simply to deny it. And if anyone thinks they can prove this claim from the Word of God, let them bring forth their strongest arguments.

* * *

Discussion Questions

(1) "No matter how much a person has attained, no matter how perfect they have become, there is still a need to *grow in grace,* and daily to advance in the knowledge and love of our Savior God." Some might read this and feel, "It's hopeless, I'll never get

there, I might as well give up." Others might say, "Hallelujah! There's always more of God to discover and experience!" How do you respond, and why?

(2) Wesley describes several stages of Christian growth.

a. In which stage would you place yourself right now?

b. Think of the most mature and complete Christian you know. Why do you think of them that way?

(3) Wesley says whether we accept the idea that real Christians don't sin must be decided not by reason or experience, but strictly by what the Bible says. Do reason or experience have any place in understanding what the Bible says?

(4) "Even those who are born again in the lowest sense, that of justification or forgiveness, do not continue in sin."

a. What does this say about those who claim to be Christians yet do continue in outward sin?

b. If forgiveness is the lowest sense of being born again, what's higher?

(5) Wesley quotes 1 John 3:8, *Everyone who commits sin is a child of the devil.* See also John 1:12, *But to all who received him [Jesus], who believed in his name, he gave power to become children of God.* What do these Bible passages say about the popular idea that everyone is a child of God?

3

"But Doesn't the Old Testament Say...?"

"But Old Testament Heroes Sinned"

In fact, there is a sort of argument which has been frequently made to support these strange claims. It's based on examples recorded in the Word of God.

"Wait a minute!" they say, "Didn't Abraham sin by lying and denying his wife?[73] Didn't Moses sin when he provoked God at the waters of strife?[74] Or to top it all off, didn't even David, the man after God's own heart,[75] commit sin in the matter of Uriah the Hittite, even the sins of murder and adultery?"[76]

Indeed he did. All this is true. But what is it you would infer from it? We can grant, first, that David, in the general course of his life, was one of the holiest people among the Jews. And we can grant, secondly, that the holiest people among the Jews did sometimes commit sin. But if you would conclude from this that all Christians do and must commit sin as long as they live, this consequence we utterly deny. It does not logically follow from those premises.

Those who make this argument seem never to have considered this declaration of our Lord: *Truly I tell you, among those born of women no one has arisen greater than John the Baptist; yet the least in the kingdom of heaven is greater than he.*[77]

I'm afraid some think "the kingdom of heaven" here means the kingdom of glory; as if the Son of God has just revealed to us that the least glorified saint in heaven is greater than anyone on earth! Just to mention this is enough to refute it. There can be do doubt that "the kingdom of heaven," here as in the following verse where it is said to be taken by force,[78] or "the kingdom of God" as St. Luke expresses it,[79] is that kingdom of God on earth to which all true believers in Christ, all real Christians, belong.

In these words, then, our Lord declares two things: first, that before he came in the flesh, no one in the whole human race had been greater than John the Baptist — which clearly means that neither Abraham nor David nor any other Jew was greater than John. Second, our Lord declares that the person who is least in the kingdom of God, that kingdom he came to set up on earth and which the violent now began to take by force, is greater than John. Not a greater prophet, as some have interpreted it, because this is clearly false on the facts of the case, but greater in the grace of God and the knowledge of our Lord Jesus Christ.

So we cannot measure the spiritual privileges of real Christians by the spiritual privileges formerly given to the Jews. We allow that their ministry or dispensation[80] was glorious, but ours exceeds in glory.[81] Anyone who would bring down the Christian dispensation to the Old Testament standard, whoever gathers up the examples of weakness recorded in the Law and the Prophets and infers from them that those who have clothed themselves with Christ[82] are given no greater strength, is sorely

27

mistaken. They *know neither the scriptures nor the power of God.*[83]

"But the Old Testament Says People Will Sin"

Someone says, "But aren't there statements in the Bible which prove the same thing, even if these examples don't show it? Doesn't the Bible say even a righteous man sins seven times a day?"

I answer, no. The Bible says no such thing. There is no such text anywhere in the Bible.

What they seem to be referring to is the sixteenth verse of the twenty-fourth chapter of Proverbs, which says, *For a righteous man may fall seven times and rise again.*[84] But that's a very different thing.

First, the words "a day" are not in the text. So if a righteous person falls seven times in their whole life, it's no more than what is said here.

Second, there is no mention of falling into sin at all. The subject here is falling into temporal affliction or trouble in this life. This is plainly seen from the verse before, which says, *Do not lie in wait like an outlaw against the home of the righteous; do no violence to the place where the righteous live.*[85] Then follows, *For a righteous man may fall seven times and rise again, but the wicked shall fall by calamity.*[86] So this verse is a warning to the wicked: "God will deliver the righteous from their trouble, but when you fall there will be no one to help you."

The objector continues: "But, even so, in other places Solomon does state plainly, *There is no one who does not sin,*[87] and, *Surely there is no one on earth so righteous as to do good without ever sinning.*"[88]

I answer, no doubt it was that way in the days of Solomon. Yes, it was that way from Adam to Moses, from Moses to Solomon, and from Solomon to Christ. In those times there was no one who did not sin. From the day sin entered the world, there was not a righteous person on earth who only did good and never sinned — until the Son of God came to take away our sins.

There's no question that *heirs, as long as they are minors, are no better than slaves, though they are the owners of all the property.*[89] This was the state of all the holy people of old, who were under the Old Testament dispensation. During that infant state of the church, they *were enslaved to the elemental spirits of the world. But when the fullness of time had come, God sent his Son, born of a woman, born under the law, in order to redeem those who were under the law, so that we might receive adoption as children*[90] — that we might receive that grace which *has now been revealed through the appearing of our Savior Christ Jesus, who abolished death and brought life and immortality to light through the gospel.*[91]

Now, therefore, we are no longer servants, but children.[92] So whatever might have been the case of those under the law of Moses, we may safely affirm with St. John that, now that the gospel has been given, *those who are born of God do not sin.*[93]

Since Pentecost, Things Are Different

It's very important to observe, much more carefully than is commonly done, the wide difference there is between the way God related to people in Old Testament times and the way he does in the Christian era. This same apostle John gives us the basis for this difference in the seventh chapter of his gospel.

After he quotes our blessed Lord as saying, *"As the scripture has said, 'Out of the believer's heart shall flow rivers of living water,'"* he immediately adds, *Now he said this about the Spirit, which believers in him were to receive; for as yet there was no Spirit, because Jesus was not yet glorified.*[94]

Now the apostle cannot mean here, as some have taught, that the miracle-working power of the Holy Spirit was not yet given, because it was; our Lord had given it to all of the apostles when he first sent them out to preach the gospel. At that time he gave them power over unclean spirits, to cast them out; power to heal the sick; indeed, power to raise the dead.[95]

But the Holy Spirit was not yet given in his ministry of helping people become holy. This came after Jesus went to heaven. It was then, when Jesus *ascended on high and made captivity a captive,* that he *gave gifts to his people,*[96] even the rebellious, that the Lord God might dwell among them.[97] And *when the day of Pentecost had come,*[98] then it was that they who waited *for the promise of the Father*[99] were made *more than conquerors*[100] over sin by the Holy Spirit who was given to them.

Peter also testifies that this great salvation from sin was not given until after Jesus was glorified in heaven.

Speaking to the brothers and sisters living at that time, he says,

You are receiving the outcome of your faith, the salvation of your souls. Then he adds, *Concerning this salvation, the prophets who prophesied of the grace that was to be yours* — that is, the working of God through grace rather than law — *made careful search and inquiry, inquiring about the person or time that the Spirit of Christ within them indicated when it testified in advance to the sufferings destined for Christ and the subsequent glory* — the glorious salvation to follow. *It was revealed to them that they were serving not themselves but you, in regard to the things that have now been announced to you through those who brought you good news by the Holy Spirit sent from heaven*[101] — at the day of Pentecost

and on to all generations, in the hearts of all true believers.

On this foundation, the grace which was brought to them by the revelation of Jesus Christ, the apostle might well base his strong exhortation: *Prepare your minds for action . . . As he who called you is holy, be holy yourselves in all your conduct.*[102]

Anyone who has duly considered these things must admit that the spiritual privileges of Christians are in no way to be measured by what the Old Testament records about those under its dispensation. Now *the fullness of time has come,*[103] the Holy Spirit has been given, the great salvation of God has been brought to humans by the revelation of Jesus Christ. The kingdom of heaven has now been set up on earth.[104] Concerning this, the Spirit of God declared long ago (in words that show that David is far from being the pattern or standard of Christian perfection), *On that day the Lord will shield the inhabitants of Jerusalem so that the feeblest among them on that day shall be like David, and the house of David shall be like God, like the angel of the Lord, at their head.*[105]

So if you want to prove that the apostle's words, *Those who are born of God do not sin,*[106] are not to be understood according to their plain, natural, obvious meaning, you will have to bring your proofs from the New Testament. Otherwise, you will be like a person *beating the air.*[107]

* * *

Discussion Questions

(1) Many people, when they hear "the kingdom of God" or "the kingdom of heaven," think only of the afterlife. Wesley insists Christians are living in the kingdom now.

a. What difference does this make in how you look at things?

b. Theologians like to say God's kingdom is "already/not yet." Would you like to learn more about that? (This author hasn't written such a study; that will be on your pastor!)

(2) Wesley makes a strong distinction between the way God worked among people before Pentecost versus since Pentecost.
a. What happened to make such a big difference?

b. How does this help you better understand how the Old and New Testaments relate to each other?

(3) Wesley is making a somewhat complicated argument in this chapter. Working as a group, how would you explain it to someone who is not in this study?

4

"But Doesn't the New Testament Say...?"

"But New Testament Heroes Sinned"

Usually, the first proof of this kind is based on actions recorded in the New Testament. "The apostles themselves," someone says, "committed sins, even the greatest of them, Peter and Paul. Paul, by his sharp argument with Barnabas;[108] and Peter by his hypocrisy at Antioch."[109]

Well, suppose both Peter and Paul did commit sin? What is it you want to prove from this? That all the other apostles committed sins sometimes? There is no shadow of proof in this.

Or would you conclude that all the other Christians of the apostolic age committed sin? Worse and worse! This is such a conclusion as, one would imagine, any person in their right mind could never have thought of.

Or will you argue it this way: "If two of the apostles did once commit sin, then all other Christians, in all ages, do and will commit sin as long as they live?" Oh, my brothers and sisters! Any child of average intelligence would be ashamed of reasoning like that.

Least of all can you, with any pretense of logic, conclude that any person *must* commit sin at all. No! God forbid we should talk that way!

No necessity of sinning was laid on the New Testament Christians. The grace of God was surely enough for them, and it is enough for us to this day. Along with the temptations that fell on them, there was a way to escape, as there is to every soul in every temptation. So no one who is tempted to any sin has to yield to it, because no one is tempted beyond their strength.[110]

Someone says, "But St. Paul asked the Lord three times, and yet he could not escape from his temptation."[111]

Let's consider his own words, literally translated:

A thorn was given me in the flesh, a messenger (literally "angel") *of Satan to torment me. Three times I appealed to the Lord about this, that it* (or "he") *would leave me, but he said to me, "My grace is sufficient for you, for power is made perfect in weakness." So, I will boast all the more gladly of my weaknesses, so that the power of Christ may dwell in me. Therefore I am content* (or "take pleasure") *with weaknesses . . . for whenever I am weak, then I am strong.*[112]

This scripture is one of the strong-holds of the supporters of sin, so let's examine it thoroughly.

We notice first that nothing indicates that this thorn, whatever it was, pushed St. Paul to sin, much less made it necessary for him to do so. So this can't be used to prove that any Christian must commit sin.

Second, the ancient fathers of the church inform us that the thorn was some kind of bodily pain. Tertullian said it was a violent headache, and Chrysostom and St. Jerome agree. St. Cyprian expresses it a little more generally, as "Many and grievous torments of the flesh and of the body."

Third, the apostle's own words exactly agree with this: *a thorn in the flesh . . . to torment* ("hit, beat, or batter") *me.*[113] And, *Power is made perfect in weakness*[114] — a word that occurs no less than four times in these two verses.

Fourth, whatever the thorn was, it could not be either inward or outward sin.

It could be neither inward thoughts nor outward expressions of pride, anger, or lust. This is clear, beyond all possible doubt, from the words that immediately follow: *So, I will boast all the more gladly of my weaknesses, so that the power of Christ may dwell in me.*[115] What, did he boast about pride, about anger, about lust? Was it through these "weaknesses" that the strength of Christ rested on him?

He goes on: *Therefore I am content with* (or "take pleasure in") *weaknesses, insults, hardships, persecutions, and calamities for the sake of Christ; for whenever I am weak, then I am strong.*[116] That is, "when I am weak in body, then I am strong in spirit."

But will anyone dare to say, "When I am weak by pride or lust, then I am strong in spirit?" I call you to bear witness today, all who feel the strength of Christ resting on you, can you boast about anger, or pride, or lust? Can you take pleasure in these infirmities? Do these weaknesses make you strong? Wouldn't you even leap into hell, if it were possible, to escape them? Judge by your own feelings, then, whether the apostle could boast about them and take pleasure in them!

Last, let's notice that this thorn was given to Paul more than fourteen years before he wrote this epistle,[117] and he wrote it several years before he finished his earthly race.[118] So after the occasion of the thorn he still had a long course to run, many battles to fight, many victories to gain, and much more to receive in all the gifts of God and the knowledge of Jesus Christ. So even if this was talking about some kind of spiritual weakness which he felt at that time, we certainly can't conclude that he was never made strong; that Paul the aged, the father in Christ, still labored under the same weaknesses; that he never attained any higher spiritual state until the day of his death.

All this goes to show that this experience of St. Paul is quite beside the question, and in no way conflicts with St. John's statement that *those who are born of God do not sin.* [119]

"But the New Testament Says People Will Sin"

"But doesn't St. James directly contradict this? He writes, *We all offend in many things.* [120] And isn't offending the same as committing sin?"

In this case, I admit it is: I admit the people spoken of here did commit sins; indeed, that they all committed many sins. But who is James speaking of here? Why, those many teachers who were not sent from God (probably the same men who taught faith without works, which James so sharply reproved in the preceding chapter), not the apostle himself, nor any real Christian.

The use of the word "we" is a common figure of speech not only in the Bible but in all kinds of writings. The apostle could not possibly include himself or any other true believer in this statement.

This is clear, first, because the same word is used in the ninth verse, where he says with our tongue we bless God and we curse people; *from the same mouth come blessing and cursing.* [121] This is true, but not out of the mouth of the apostle, nor of anyone who is a new creation in Christ.[122]

Second, this is clear from the verse just before the one we are discussing, and obviously connected with it: *My brethren, let not many of you become teachers, knowing that we shall receive a greater condemnation. For we all offend in many things.*[123] "We!" Who? Not the apostles, not true believers. This is talking about those who know they should receive a greater condemnation, because of those many offenses. But this could not be said of the apostle himself, or of any who followed in his steps, because *there is no condemnation to those who do not walk according to the flesh, but according to the Spirit.*[124]

Third, the rest of that very verse itself proves that "we all offend" cannot mean either all people, or all Christians, because it immediately continues by mentioning someone who does not offend, as the "we" first mentioned does. This second person is clearly different from "we," and indeed is called perfect.[125]

So James clearly explains himself, and fixes the meaning of his own words. And in case anyone remains unconvinced, John, writing many years after James, puts the matter entirely beyond dispute by the statements we already considered.

But here a fresh difficulty may arise: How do we reconcile St. John with himself? On one hand he says, *Those who have been born of God do not sin,*[126] and two chapters later, *We know that those who are born of God do not sin.*[127] On the other hand, he says, *If we say that we have no sin, we deceive ourselves, and the truth is not in us,*[128] and, *If we say that we have not sinned, we make him a liar, and his word is not in us.*[129]

As great a difficulty as this may at first appear, it vanishes away if we observe three things.

First, in chapter one, the tenth verse fixes the meaning of the eighth. "If we say we have no sin" in eight is explained by "If we say we have not sinned" in ten.

Second, the question under consideration is not whether we have or have not sinned in the past, but whether we do sin, whether we commit sin now. Neither of these verses says we do.

Third, verse nine explains both verses eight and ten: *If we confess our sins, he who is faithful and just will forgive us our sins and cleanse us from all unrighteousness.*[130]

In other words, John says, "I have said before that the blood of Jesus cleanses us from all sin. Let no one say they don't need it, thinking they have no sin to be cleansed from. If we say we have no sin or that we have not sinned, we deceive ourselves and call God a liar. But if we confess our sins, he is faithful and just, and will not only forgive our sins but also cleanse us from all unrighteousness, so we can *go and sin no more.*"[131]

John, therefore, is quite consistent with himself, as well as with the other holy writers.

This will be even clearer if we look at everything he says about this matter in one place. He says:

1. The blood of Jesus Christ cleanses us from all sin.[132]
2. No one can say, "I have not sinned, I have no sin to be cleansed from."[133]
3. But God is ready both to forgive our past sins and to save us from them for the time to come.[134]
4. The apostle adds, *I am writing these things to you so that you may not sin. But if anyone does sin* (it can also be translated "if anyone has sinned"), they don't have to continue in sin, because, *we have an advocate with the Father, Jesus Christ the righteous.*[135]

So far this is all clear. But just in case any doubt might remain on a point of such vast importance, the apostle resumes this subject in the third chapter of this epistle, and again explains his meaning:

Little children, let no one deceive you (into thinking I have given any encouragement to those who continue in sin). *Everyone who does what is right is righteous, just as he* (God) *is righteous. Everyone who commits sin is a child of the devil; for the devil has been sinning from the beginning. The Son of God was revealed for this purpose, to destroy the works of the devil. Those who have been born of God do not sin, because God's seed abides in them; they cannot sin, because they have been born of God. The children of God and the children of the devil are revealed in this way.* [136]

Here, just in case there might possibly have remained some doubt in weak minds, the last of the inspired writers purposely settles the point, and in the clearest possible way.

Therefore, in keeping both with the teaching of John and with the whole direction of the New Testament, we fix this conclusion: A Christian is so far perfect as to not commit sin. This is the glorious privilege of every Christian, even those who are still infants in Christ. [137]

* * *

Discussion Questions

(1) In this chapter Wesley corrects popular misquotations or misunderstandings of well-known Bible passages.

a. How many sayings can you think of that many people believe are in the Bible but really aren't?

b. What Bible passages do some people misuse, either to excuse their behavior or to manipulate other people?

c. What does all this tell you about the importance of Bible study?

(2) Wesley goes to great lengths to show that the Bible does not contradict itself. Why is this important?

(3) "We fix this conclusion: A Christian is so far perfect as to not commit sin. This is the glorious privilege of every Christian, even those who are still infants in Christ." Use Wesley's own style of word-for-word argument to answer:

a. By this statement, is Wesley saying that anyone who commits a sin must not be a Christian?

b. Is he saying that anyone who commits a sin ceases to be a Christian?

c. In your own words, what is Wesley saying?

5

Free Inside

Even babies in Christ are perfect in the first sense, that of not committing outward sins. But only those who are strong in the Lord and *have conquered the evil one*, those who *know God who is from the beginning,*[138] are perfect in the second sense: being free from evil thoughts and attitudes.

Christians Are Free From Sinful Thoughts

First, they are free from evil or sinful thoughts.

Let's start by observing that thoughts about evil are not always evil thoughts. A thought concerning sin, and a sinful thought, are widely different.

For instance, someone might think about a murder someone committed. That is not an evil or sinful thought. Our blessed Lord himself no doubt thought about or understood what the devil was saying when he promised, *All these I will give you, if you will fall down and worship me.*[139] But he had no evil or sinful thought; indeed, he was not capable of having one. It follows, then, that real Christians don't have evil or sinful thoughts either, because *everyone who is fully qualified will be like their teacher.*[140] So if Jesus their teacher was free from evil or sinful thoughts, they are, too.

Indeed, where would evil thoughts come from, in those who are like their teacher? Evil thoughts come from the heart if they come at all.[141] If someone's heart is no longer evil, then evil thoughts can no longer come from it. If a tree is diseased, the fruit will be, too. But in this case, the tree is good. Therefore, the fruit is good, also, because Jesus said, *In the same way, every good tree bears good fruit, but the bad tree bears bad fruit. A good tree cannot bear bad fruit, nor can a bad tree bear good fruit.*[142]

St. Paul affirms from his own experience this same happy privilege of real Christians. *For the weapons of our warfare are not merely human, but they have divine power to destroy strongholds. We destroy arguments* — the original Greek word signifies all the reasonings of pride and unbelief against the declarations, promises, or gifts of God — *and every proud obstacle raised up against the knowledge of God, and we take every thought captive to obey Christ.*[143]

Christians Are Free From Evil Attitudes

Second, in the same way Christians are freed from evil thoughts, they are also freed from evil attitudes.

This can be seen from the words of Jesus already quoted: *A disciple is not above the teacher, but everyone who is fully qualified will be like the teacher.*[144]

He had just been delivering some of the noblest teachings of Christianity, and some of the most painful to flesh and blood. *I say to you, love your enemies, do good to those who hate you . . . If anyone strikes you on the cheek, offer the other also.*[145]

He knew very well that the world would not receive these, so he immediately adds, *Can a blind person guide a blind person? Will not both fall into a pit?*[146] In other words, "Don't consult with flesh and blood about these things — with people who have no spiritual discernment,[147] people whose understanding God has not opened — or else they and you might perish together."

Wise fools always raise two big objections at this point: "Nobody can live up to that, it's too hard!" Or, "He's just preaching an unrealistic ideal." In the next verse Jesus removes those objections. *"A disciple is not above the teacher* — therefore, if I have suffered, be content to walk in my footsteps, and have no doubt that I will fulfill my promise — *but everyone who is fully qualified will be like the teacher."*[148] The teacher was free from all sinful attitudes, therefore his followers, every real, fully qualified Christian, will be free from them as well.

Every one of these real Christians can say with St. Paul, *I have been crucified with Christ; and it is no longer I who live, but it is Christ who lives in me.*[149] These words clearly describe a deliverance from inward as well as outward sin. This is expressed both in the negative, *it is no longer I who live* — my evil nature, which gives sin its form, is destroyed; and in the positive, *it is Christ who lives in me* — what is living in me is everything holy and just and good. Indeed, the two expressions, "Christ lives in me" and "I no longer live," are inseparably connected, because *What agreement does Christ have with Beliar?*[150]

Christians Have Pure Hearts

Christ, who lives in true believers, has cleansed their hearts by faith.[151] All who have *Christ in you, the hope of glory*[152] purify *themselves, just as he is pure.*[153]

They are purified from pride, for Christ was humble in heart.[154]

They are purified from self-will or selfishness, for Christ desired only to do the will of his Father and to finish his work.[155]

They are purified from anger, in the common sense of the word, for Christ was meek and gentle,[156] patient and long-suffering.

I say, "in the common sense of the word," for not all anger is evil. We read of our Lord himself that he once looked around in anger. But with what kind of anger? The next phrase shows us: *he was grieved at their hardness of heart.*[157] So then he was angry at the sin, and at the same time grieved for the sinners; angry or displeased at the offense, but sorry for the offenders. With anger, yes, with hatred, he looked at the thing, but with grief and love he looked at the persons. *Go,* you who are perfect, *and do likewise.*[158] In this way *be angry but do not sin.*[159] Feel offended at every offense against God, but only love and tender compassion for the offender.

So this is how Jesus saves his people from their sins.[160] And not only from outward sins, but also from the sins of their hearts, from evil thoughts and evil attitudes.

You Don't Have to Wait Until You Die

"True," some say, "we will be saved from our sins, outward and inward; but not until death, not in this world."

But how can you reconcile that with this clear statement of St. John? *Love has been perfected among us in this: that we may have boldness on the day of judgment, because as he is, so are we in this world.*[161]

No one can deny that the apostle here speaks of himself and other living Christians. As if he had foreseen this very evasion, and set himself to overturn it from the beginning, he flatly affirms that not only at or after death, but *in this world,* they are as their Lord.

This is in exact agreement with his words in the first chapter of this epistle: *God is light and in him there is no darkness at all . . . If we walk in the light as he himself is in the light, we have fellowship with one another, and the blood of Jesus his Son cleanses us from all sin.* [162] And again: *If we confess our sins, he who is faithful and just will forgive us our sins and cleanse us from all unrighteousness.* [163]

Now it's clear that the apostle here also speaks of a deliverance worked *in this world.* In verse 7, he doesn't say the blood of Christ "will cleanse" us at the hour of death, or in the day of judgment. He says *cleanses,* at the present time, *us,* living Christians, *from all sin.* [164] It's equally clear that if any sin remains, we are not cleansed *from all sin.* If any unrighteousness remains in the soul, it is not cleansed *from all unrighteousness.*

Let no one sin against their own soul by saying that this only relates to justification, or to cleansing us from the guilt of sin. [165] This is wrong for two reasons. First, because this is mixing together what the apostle clearly makes separate when he first says *will forgive us our sins,* and then says *and cleanse us from all unrighteousness.* [166]

The second reason this is wrong is because this is asserting, in the strongest sense possible, the false doctrine of justification by works. [167] It is saying that we cannot be forgiven until we are completely holy, both inwardly and outwardly; because if the cleansing *from all sin* John speaks of in verse 7 refers only to cleansing from the guilt of sin, then the only way we can be cleansed from that guilt, or justified, is to already be walking in the light as Jesus is in the light.[168]

So what we are left with is this: Christians are saved in this world from all sin and from all unrighteousness. They are now perfect in this sense: they do not commit sin, and they are free from evil thoughts and attitudes.

The Prophets Knew

In this way the Lord has fulfilled the things he spoke through his holy prophets, things which have been since the world began.

For example, through Moses, saying, *[I] will circumcise your heart and the heart of your descendants, so that you will love the Lord your God with all your heart and with all your soul.*[169]

And through David, crying out, *Create in me a clean heart, O God, and put a new and right spirit within me.*[170]

And most remarkably through Ezekiel, in these words:

I will sprinkle clean water upon you, and you shall be clean from all your uncleannesses, and from all your idols I will cleanse you. A new heart I will give you, and a new spirit I will put within you . . . and make you follow my statutes and be careful to observe my ordinances . . . Thus says the Lord God: On the day that I cleanse you from all your iniquities . . . the nations that are left all around you shall know that I, the Lord, have rebuilt the ruined places . . . I, the Lord, have spoken, and I will do it.[171]

Press On to the Promise

Since we have these promises, beloved, both in the Law and in the Prophets, and having the prophetic word confirmed to us in the Gospel[172] by our blessed Lord and his apostles, *let us cleanse ourselves from every defilement of body and of spirit, making holiness perfect in the fear of God.* [173]

Those who enter God's rest also cease from their labors. [174] *Therefore, while the promise of entering his rest is still open, let us take care that none of you should seem to have failed to reach it.* [175]

This one thing let us do: forgetting what lies behind and straining forward to what lies ahead, let us press on toward the goal for the prize of the heavenly call of God in Christ Jesus, [176] crying unto him day and night, until we also are *set free from the bondage to decay* and *obtain the freedom of the glory of the children of God!* [177]

* * *

Discussion Questions

(1) When bad thoughts come into your mind, what practical steps can you take to take them *captive to obey Christ* and replace them with godly thoughts?

(2) Wesley says the key to freedom from evil attitudes is in St. Paul's statement, *I have been crucified with Christ; and it is no longer I who live, but it is Christ who lives in me.* [178] What does that mean to you?

(3) Wesley writes, "With anger, yes, with hatred, he [Jesus] looked at the thing [sin], but with grief and love he looked at the persons." Today "love the sinner but hate the sin" has become a controversial phrase in some circles. What do you think about it?

47

(4) Wesley's message of Christian perfection is often summarized as saying that every Christian can and should, through the Holy Spirit, reach a state where one is not consciously committing any sin, and everything one does is motivated by love. Does this adequately sum up the message of this sermon?

(5) Can you identify something you have done, said, or thought today that you know is sinful? Can you avoid it tomorrow?

(6) What specific steps can you take this week, with the help of the Holy Spirit, to eliminate conscious sins from your life?

(7) What specific steps can you take this week, with the help of the Holy Spirit, to eliminate non-loving thoughts, attitudes, and motives from your life?

(8) What is the most important thing you have learned from this study?

Extra Credit

1. Sing Charles Wesley's hymn, found in Appendix 2, to the tune of "Amazing Grace." Did it help you understand the message?
2. Leave a review of this study wherever you purchased it to help others find it.

6

Appendix 1: Wesley's Original Words

Christian Perfection

By John Wesley
    Sermon 40
    Text from the 1872 edition - Thomas Jackson, editor

Not as though I had already attained, either were already perfect.
Philippians 3:12

1. There is scarce any expression in Holy Writ which has given more offence than this. The word *perfect* is what many cannot bear. The very sound of it is an abomination to them. And whosoever *preaches perfection* (as the phrase is,) that is, asserts that it is attainable in this life, runs great hazard of being accounted by them worse than a heathen man or a publican.

2. And hence some have advised, wholly to lay aside the use of those expressions, "because they have given so great

offence." But are they not found in the oracles of God? If so, by what authority can any Messenger of God lay them aside, even though all men should be offended? We have not so learned Christ; neither may we thus give place to the devil. Whatsoever God hath Spoken that will we speak, whether men will hear or whether they will forbear; knowing that then alone can any Minister of Christ be "pure from the blood of all men," when he hath "not shunned to declare unto them all the counsel of God." [Acts 20:26, 27]

3. We may not, therefore, lay these expressions aside, seeing they are the words of God, and not of man. But we may and ought to explain the meaning of them, that those who are sincere of heart may not err to the right hand or to the left, from the mark of the prize of their high calling. And this is the more needful to be done because in the verse already repeated the Apostle speaks of himself as not perfect: "Not," saith he, "as though I were already perfect." And yet immediately after, in the fifteenth verse, he speaks of himself, yea and many others, as perfect. "Let us," saith he, "as many as be perfect, be thus minded." [Phil. 3:15]

4. In order, therefore, to remove the difficulty arising from this seeming contradiction, as well as to give light to them who are pressing forward to the mark, and that those who are lame be not turned out of the way, I shall endeavor to show,

I. First, in what sense Christians are not; and,
  II. Secondly, in what sense they are, perfect.

I.

1. In the first place I shall endeavor to show in what sense Christians are *not perfect*. And both from experience and Scripture it appears, First, that they are not perfect in knowledge: they are not *so* perfect in this life as to be free from ignorance. They know, it may be, in common with other men, many things relating to the present world; and they know, with regard to the world to come, the general truths which God hath revealed. They know, likewise, (what the natural man receiveth not, for these things are spiritually discerned,) "what manner of love" it is wherewith "the Father" hath loved them, "that they should be called the sons of God." [1 John 3:1] They know the mighty working of his Spirit in their hearts; [Eph. 3:16] and the wisdom of his providence, directing all their paths, [Prov. 3:6] and causing all things to work together for their good. [Rom. 8:28] Yea, they know in every circumstance of life what the Lord requireth of them, and how to keep a conscience void of offence both toward God and toward man. [Acts 24:16]

2. But innumerable are the things which they know not. Touching the Almighty himself, they cannot search him out to perfection. "Lo, these are but a part of his ways; but the thunder of his power who can understand?" [Job 26:14] They cannot understand, I will not say, how "there are Three that bear record in heaven, the Father, the Son, and the Holy Spirit, and these three are one;" [1 John 5:7] or how the eternal Son of God "took upon himself the form of a servant;" [Phil. 2:7] — but not any one attribute, not any one circumstance of the divine nature. [2 Pet. 1:4] Neither is it for them to know the times and seasons [Acts 1:7] when God will work his great works upon the

earth; no, not even those which he hath in part revealed by his servants and Prophets since the world began. [see Amos 3:7] Much less do they know when God, having "accomplished the number of his elect, will hasten his kingdom;" when "the heavens shall pass away with a great noise, and the elements shall melt with fervent heat." [2 Pet. 3:10]

3. They know not the reasons even of many of his present dispensations with the sons of men; but are constrained to rest here, — Though "clouds and darkness are round about him, righteousness and judgment are the habitation of his seat." [Ps. 97:2] Yea, often with regard to his dealings with themselves, doth their Lord say unto them, "What I do, thou knowest not now; but thou shalt know hereafter." [John 13:7] And how little do they know of what is ever before them, of even the visible works of his hands! — How "he spreadeth the north over the empty place, and hangeth the earth upon nothing?" [Job 26:7] How he unites all the parts of this vast machine by a secret chain which cannot be broken? So great is the ignorance, so very little the knowledge, of even the best of men!

4. No one, then, is so perfect in this life, as to be free from ignorance. Nor, Secondly, from mistake; which indeed is almost an unavoidable consequence of it; seeing those who "know but in part" [1 Cor. 13:12] are ever liable to err touching the things which they know not. It is true, the children of God do not mistake as to the things essential to salvation: They do not "put darkness for light, or light for darkness;" [Isa. 5:20] neither "seek death in the error of their life." [Wisdom 1:12] For they are "taught of God," and the way which he teaches them, the way of holiness,

is so plain, that "the wayfaring man, though a fool, need not err therein." [Isa. 35:8] But in things unessential to salvation they do err, and that frequently. The best and wisest of men are frequently mistaken even with regard to facts; believing those things not to have been which really were, or those to have been done which were not. Or, suppose they are not mistaken as to the fact itself, they may be with regard to its circumstances; believing them, or many of them, to have been quite different from what in truth, they were. And hence cannot but arise many farther mistakes. Hence they may believe either past or present actions which were or are evil, to be good; and such as were or are good, to be evil. Hence also they may judge not according to truth with regard to the characters of men; and that, not only by supposing good men to be better, or wicked men to be worse, than they are, but by believing them to have been or to be good men who were or are very wicked; or perhaps those to have been or to be wicked men, who were or are holy and unreprovable.

5. Nay, with regard to the Holy Scriptures themselves, as careful as they are to avoid it, the best of men are liable to mistake, and do mistake day by day; especially with respect to those parts thereof which less immediately relate to practice. Hence even the children of God are not agreed as to the interpretation of many places in holy writ: Nor is their difference of opinion any proof that they are not the children of God on either side; but it is a proof that we are no more to expect any living man to be infallible than to be omniscient.

6. If it be objected to what has been observed under this and the preceding head, that St. John, speaking to his brethren

in the faith says, "Ye have an unction from the Holy One, and ye know all things:" (1 John 2:20) The answer is plain: "Ye know all things that are needful for your souls' health." [cf. 3 John 2] That the Apostle never designed to extend this farther, that he could not speak it in an absolute sense, is clear, First from hence; — that otherwise he would describe the disciple as "above his Master;" seeing Christ himself, as man, knew not all things: "Of that hour," saith he, "knoweth no man; no, not the Son, but the Father only." [Mark 13:32] It is clear, Secondly, from the Apostle's own words that follow: "These things have I written unto you concerning them that deceive you;" [cf. 1 John 3:7] as well as from his frequently repeated caution, "Let no man deceive you;" [see Mark 13:5; Eph. 5:6; 2 Thess. 2:3] which had been altogether needless, had not those very persons who had that unction from the Holy One [1 John 2:20] been liable, not to ignorance only, but to mistake also.

7. Even Christians, therefore, are not *so* perfect as to be free either from ignorance or error: We may, Thirdly, add, nor from infirmities. — Only let us take care to understand this word aright: Only let us not give that soft title to known sins, as the manner of some is. So, one man tells us, "Every man has his infirmity, and mine is drunkenness;" Another has the infirmity of uncleanness; another of taking God's holy name in vain; and yet another has the infirmity of calling his brother, "Thou fool," [Matt. 5:22] or returning "railing for railing." [1 Pet. 3:9] It is plain that all you who thus speak, if ye repent not, shall, with your infirmities, go quick into hell! But I mean hereby, not only those which are properly termed *bodily infirmities*, but all those inward or outward imperfections which are not of a moral nature.

Such are the weakness or slowness of understanding, dullness or confusedness of apprehension, incoherency of thought, irregular quickness or heaviness of imagination. Such (to mention no more of this kind) is the want of a ready or of a retentive memory. Such in another kind, are those which are commonly, in some measure, consequent upon these; namely, slowness of speech, impropriety of language, ungracefulness of pronunciation; to which one might add a thousand nameless defects, either in conversation or behaviour. These are the infirmities which are found in the best of men, in a larger or smaller proportion. And from these none can hope to be perfectly freed till the spirit returns to God that gave it. [Eccles. 12:7]

8. Nor can we expect, till then, to be wholly free from temptation. Such perfection belongeth not to this life. It is true, there are those who, being given up to work all uncleanness with greediness, [Eph. 4:19] scarce perceive the temptations which they resist not, and so seem to be without temptation. There are also many whom the wise enemy of souls, seeing to be fast asleep in the dead form of godliness, will not tempt to gross sin, lest they should awake before they drop into everlasting burnings. I know there are also children of God who, being now justified freely, [Rom. 5:1] having found redemption in the blood of Christ, [Eph. 1:7] for the present feel no temptation. God hath said to their enemies, "Touch not mine anointed, and do my children no harm." [See 1 Chron. 16:22] And for this season, it may be for weeks or months, he causeth them to "ride on high places;" [Deut. 32:13] he beareth them as on eagles' wings, [Exod. 19:4] above all the fiery

darts of the wicked one. [Eph. 6:16] But this state will not last always; as we may learn from that single consideration, — that the Son of God himself, in the days of his flesh, was tempted even to the end of his life. [Heb. 2:18; 4:15; 6:7] Therefore, so let his servant expect to be; for "it is enough that he be as his Master." [Luke 6:40]

9. Christian perfection, therefore, does not imply (as some men seem to have imagined) an exemption either from ignorance or mistake, or infirmities or temptations. Indeed, it is only another term for holiness. They are two names for the same thing. Thus every one that is perfect is holy, and every one that is holy is, in the Scripture sense, perfect. Yet we may, lastly, observe, that neither in this respect is there any absolute perfection on earth. There is no *perfection of degrees*, as it is termed; none which does not admit of a continual increase. So that how much soever any man hath attained, or in how high a degree soever he is perfect, he hath still need to "grow in grace," [2 Pet. 3:18] and daily to advance in the knowledge and love of God his Saviour. [see Phil. 1:9]

II.

1. In what sense, then, are Christians perfect? This is what I shall endeavor, in the Second place, to show. But it should be premised, that there are several stages in Christian life, as in natural; some of the children of God being but newborn babes; others having attained to more maturity. And accordingly St. John, in his first Epistle, (1 John 2:12, &c.) applies himself severally to those he terms little children,

those he styles young men, and those whom he entitles fathers. "I write unto you, little children," saith the Apostle, "because your sins are forgiven you:" Because thus far you have attained, — being "justified freely," you "have peace with God, through Jesus Christ." [Rom. 5:1] "I write unto you, young men, because ye have overcome the wicked one;" or (as he afterwards addeth,) "because ye are strong, and the word of God abideth in you." [1 John 2:13, 14] Ye have quenched the fiery darts of the wicked one, [Eph. 6:16] the doubts and fears wherewith he disturbed your first peace; and the witness of God, that your sins are forgiven, now abideth in your heart. "I write unto you, fathers, because ye have known him that is from the beginning." [1 John 2:13] Ye have known both the Father and the Son and the Spirit of Christ, in your inmost soul. Ye are "perfect men, being grown up to the measure of the stature of the fulness of Christ." [Eph. 4:13]

2. It is of these chiefly I speak in the latter part of this discourse: For these only are properly Christians. But even babes in Christ are in such a sense perfect, or born of God, (an expression taken also in divers senses,) as, First, not to commit sin. If any doubt of this privilege of the sons of God, the question is not to be decided by abstract reasonings, which may be drawn out into an endless length, and leave the point just as it was before. Neither is it to be determined by the experience of this or that particular person. Many may suppose they do not commit sin, when they do; but this proves nothing either way. To the law and to the testimony we appeal. "Let God be true, and every man a liar." [Rom. 3:4] By his Word will we abide, and that alone. Hereby we ought to be judged.

3. Now the Word of God plainly declares, that even those who are justified, who are born again in the lowest sense, "do not continue in sin;" that they cannot "live any longer therein;" (Rom. 6:1, 2) that they are "planted together in the likeness of the death" of Christ; (Rom. 6:5) that their "old man is crucified with him," the body of sin being destroyed, so that henceforth they do not serve sin; that being dead with Christ, they are free from sin; (Rom. 6:6, 7) that they are "dead unto sin, and alive unto God;" (Rom. 6:11) that "sin hath no more dominion over them," who are "not under the law, but under grace;" but that these, "being free from sin, are become the servants of righteousness." (Rom. 6:14, 18)

4. The very least which can be implied in these words, is, that the persons spoken of therein, namely, all real Christians, or believers in Christ, are made free from outward sin. And the same freedom, which St. Paul here expresses in such variety of phrases, St. Peter expresses in that one: (1 Pet. 4:1, 2) "He that hath suffered in the flesh hath ceased from sin, — that he no longer should live to the desires of men, but to the will of God." For this *ceasing from sin*, if it be interpreted in the lowest sense, as regarding only the outward behaviour, must denote the ceasing from the outward act, from any outward transgression of the law.

5. But most express are the well-known words of St. John, in the third chapter of his First Epistle, verse 8, &c.: "He that committeth sin is of the devil; for the devil sinneth from the beginning. For this purpose the Son of God was manifested, that he might destroy the works of the devil. Whosoever is born of God doth not commit sin; for his seed remaineth in him: And he cannot sin because he is

born of God." [1 John 3:8, 9] And those in the fifth: (1 John 5:18) "We know that whosoever is born of God sinneth not; but he that is begotten of God keepeth himself, and that wicked one toucheth him not."

6. Indeed it is said this means only, He sinneth not *wilfully*; or he doth not commit sin *habitually*; or, *not as other men do*; or, *not as he did before.* But by whom is this said? By St.John? No. There is no such word in the text; nor in the whole chapter; nor in all his Epistle; nor in any part of his writings whatsoever. Why then, the best way to answer a bold assertion is simply to deny it. And if any man can prove it from the Word of God, let him bring forth his strong reasons.

7. And a sort of reason there is, which has been frequently brought to support these strange assertions, drawn from the examples recorded in the Word of God: "What!" say they, "did not Abraham himself commit sin, — prevaricating, and denying his wife? Did not Moses commit sin, when he provoked God at the waters of strife? Nay, to produce one for all, did not even David, 'the man after God's own heart,' commit sin, in the matter of Uriah the Hittite; even murder and adultery?" It is most sure he did. All this is true. But what is it you would infer from hence? It may be granted, First, that David, in the general course of his life, was one of the holiest men among the Jews; and, Secondly, that the holiest men among the Jews did sometimes commit sin. But if you would hence infer, that all Christians do and must commit sin as long as they live; this consequence we utterly deny: It will never follow from those premises.

8. Those who argue thus, seem never to have considered that

declaration of our Lord: (Matt. 11:11) "Verily I say unto you, Among them that are born of women there hath not risen a greater than John the Baptist: Notwithstanding he that is least in the kingdom of heaven is greater than he." I fear, indeed, there are some who have imagined "the kingdom of heaven," here, to mean the kingdom of glory; as if the Son of God had just discovered to us, that the least glorified saint in heaven is greater than any man upon earth! To mention this is sufficiently to refute it. There can, therefore, no doubt be made, but "the kingdom of heaven," here, (as in the following verse, where it is said to be taken by force.) [Matt. 11:12] or, "the kingdom of God," as St. Luke expresses it, — is that kingdom of God on earth whereunto all true believers in Christ, all real Christians, belong. In these words, then, our Lord declares two things: First, that before his coming in the flesh, among all the children of men there had not been one greater than John the Baptist; whence it evidently follows, that neither Abraham, David, nor any Jew was greater than John. Our Lord, Secondly, declares that he which is least in the kingdom of God (in that kingdom which he came to set up on earth, and which the violent now began to take by force) is greater than he: — Not a greater Prophet as some have interpreted the word; for this is palpably false in fact; but greater in the grace of God, and the knowledge of our Lord Jesus Christ. Therefore, we cannot measure the privileges of real Christians by those formerly given to the Jews. Their "ministration," (or dispensation,) we allow "was glorious;" but ours "exceeds in glory." [2 Cor. 3:7-9] So that whosoever would bring down the Christian dispensation to the Jewish standard, whosoever gleans up the examples of weakness, recorded in the Law and the Prophets, and thence infers that they who have "put on Christ" [Gal. 3:27] are endued with no greater strength, doth greatly err, neither "knowing the Scriptures, nor the power of God." [Matt. 22:29]

9. "But are there not assertions in Scripture which prove the same thing, if it cannot be inferred from those examples? Does not the Scripture say expressly, "Even a just man sinneth seven times a day?" I answer, No. The Scripture says no such thing. There is no such text in all the Bible. That which seems to be intended is the sixteenth verse of the twenty-fourth chapter of the Proverbs the words of which are these: "A just man falleth seven times, and riseth up again." [Prov. 24:16] But this is quite another thing. For, First, the words "a day" are not in the text. So that if a just man falls seven times in his life, it is as much as is affirmed here. Secondly, here is no mention of *falling into sin* at all; what is here mentioned is *falling into temporal affliction*. This plainly appears from the verse before, the words of which are these: "Lay not wait, O wicked man, against the dwelling of the righteous; spoil not his resting place." [Prov. 24:15] It follows, "For a just man falleth seven times, and riseth up again; but the wicked shall fall into mischief." As if he had said, "God will deliver him out of his trouble; but when thou fallest, there shall be none to deliver thee."

10. "But, however, in other places," continue the objectors, "Solomon does assert plainly, 'There is no man that sinneth not;' (1 Kings 8:46; 2 Chron. 6:36) yea, "There is not a just man upon earth that doeth good, and sinneth not.' (Eccles. 7:20.)" I answer, Without doubt, thus it was in the days of Solomon. Yea, thus it was from Adam to Moses, from

Moses to Solomon, and from Solomon to Christ. There was then no man that sinned not. Even from the day that sin entered into the world, there was not a just man upon earth that did good and sinned not, until the Son of God was manifested to take away our sins. It is unquestionably true, that "the heir, as long as he is a child, differeth nothing from a servant." [Gal. 4:1] And that even so they (all the holy men of old, who were under the Jewish dispensation) were, during that infant state of the Church, "in bondage under the elements of the world." [Gal. 4:3] "But when the fulness of the time was come, God sent forth his Son, made under the law, to redeem them that were under the law, that they might receive the adoption of sons;" [Gal. 4:4] — that they might receive that "grace which is now made manifest by the appearing of our Saviour, Jesus Christ, who hath abolished death, and brought life and immortality to light through the gospel." (2 Tim. 1:10) Now, therefore, they "are no more servants, but sons." [see Gal. 4:7] So that, whatsoever was the case of those under the law, we may safely affirm with St. John, that, since the gospel was given, "he that is born of God sinneth not." [1 John 5:18]

11. It is of great importance to observe, and that more carefully than is commonly done, the wide difference there is between the Jewish and the Christian dispensation; and that ground of it which the same Apostle assigns in the seventh chapter of his Gospel. (John 7:38, &c.) After he had there related, those words of our blessed Lord, "He that believeth on me, as the Scripture hath said, out of his belly shall flow rivers of living water," he immediately subjoins, "This spake he of the Spirit," *ou emellon lambanein hoi pisteuontes eis auton, — which they who should believe*

on him were afterwards to receive. For the Holy Ghost was not yet given, because that Jesus was not yet glorified." [John 7:39] Now, the Apostle cannot mean here, (as some have taught,) that the miracle-working power of the Holy Ghost was not yet given. For this was given; our Lord had given it to all the Apostles, when he first sent them forth to preach the gospel. He then gave them power over unclean spirits to cast them out; power to heal the sick; yea, to raise the dead. [Mark 10:8] But the Holy Ghost was not yet given in his sanctifying graces, as he was after Jesus was glorified. It was then when "he ascended up on high, and led captivity captive," that he "received" those "gifts for men, yea, even for the rebellious, that the Lord God might dwell among them." [Ps. 68:18; cf. Eph. 4:8] And when the day of Pentecost was fully come, [Acts 2:1] then first it was, that they who "waited for the promise of the Father" [Acts 1:4] were made more than conquerors [Rom. 8:37] over sin by the Holy Ghost given unto them.

12. That this great salvation from sin was not given till Jesus was glorified, St. Peter also plainly testifies; where, speaking of his brethren in the flesh, as now "receiving the end of their faith, the salvation of their souls," he adds, (1 Peter 1:9, 10, &c.) "Of which salvation the Prophets have inquired and searched diligently, who prophesied of the grace" that is, the gracious dispensation, "that should come unto you: Searching what, or what manner of time the Spirit of Christ which was in them did signify, when it testified beforehand the sufferings of Christ. And the glory," the glorious salvation, "that should follow. Unto whom it was revealed, that not unto themselves, but unto us they did minister the things which are now reported

unto you by them that have preached the gospel unto you with the Holy Ghost sent down from heaven;" [1 Pet. 1:12] viz., at the day of Pentecost, and so unto all generations, into the hearts of all true believers. On this ground, even "the grace which was brought unto them by the revelation of Jesus Christ," [1 Pet. 1:13] the Apostle might well build that strong exhortation, "Wherefore girding up the loins of your mind, — as he which hath called you is holy, so be ye holy in all manner of conversation." [1 Pet. 1:13]

13. Those who have duly considered these things must allow, that the privileges of Christians are in no wise to be measured by what the Old Testament records concerning those who were under the Jewish dispensation; seeing the fulness of times is now come; the Holy Ghost is now given; the great salvation of God is brought unto men, by the revelation of Jesus Christ. The kingdom of heaven is now set up on earth; concerning which the Spirit of God declared of old, (so far is David from being the pattern or standard of Christian perfection,) "He that is feeble among them at that day, shall be as David; and the house of David shall be as God, as the angel of the Lord before them." (Zech. 12:8)

14. If, therefore, you would prove that the Apostle's words, "He that is born of God sinneth not," [1 John 5:18] are not to be understood according to their plain, natural, obvious meaning, it is from the New Testament you are to bring your proofs, else you will fight as one that beateth the air. [1 Cor. 9:26] And the first of these which is usually brought is taken from the examples recorded in the New Testament. "The Apostles themselves," it is said, "committed sin; nay, the greatest of them, Peter and Paul: St. Paul, by his sharp

contention with Barnabas; [Acts 15:39] and St. Peter, by his dissimulation at Antioch." [Gal. 2:11] Well: Suppose both Peter and Paul did then commit sin; what is it you would infer from hence? That all the other Apostles committed sin sometimes? There is no shadow of proof in this. Or would you thence infer, that all the other Christians of the apostolic age committed sin? Worse and worse: This is such an inference as, one would imagine, a man in his senses could never have thought of. Or will you argue thus: "If two of the Apostles did once commit sin, then all other Christians, in all ages, do and will commit sin as long as they live?" Alas, my brother! a child of common understanding would be ashamed of such reasoning as this. Least of all can you with any colour of argument infer, that any man *must* commit sin at all. No: God forbid we should thus speak! No necessity of sinning was laid upon them. The grace of God was surely sufficient for them. And it is sufficient for us at this day. With the temptation which fell on them, there was a way to escape; as there is to every soul of man in every temptation. So that whosoever is tempted to any sin, need not yield; for no man is tempted above that he is able to bear. [1 Cor. 10:13]

15. "But St. Paul besought the Lord thrice, and yet he could not escape from his temptation." Let us consider his own words literally translated: "There was given to me a thorn to the flesh, an angel" (or messenger) "of Satan, to buffet me. Touching this, I besought the Lord thrice, that it" (or he) "might depart from me. And he said unto me, My grace is sufficient for thee: For my strength is made perfect in weakness. Most gladly, therefore, will I rather glory in" these "my weaknesses, that the strength of Christ may rest

upon me. Therefore I take pleasure in weaknesses; — for when I am weak, then am I strong." [2 Cor. 12:7-10]

16. As this scripture is one of the strong-holds of the patrons of sin, it may be proper to weigh it thoroughly. Let it be observed then, First, it does by no means appear that this thorn, whatsoever it was, occasioned St. Paul to commit sin; much less laid him under any necessity of doing so. Therefore, from hence it can never be proved that any Christian must commit sin. Secondly, the ancient Fathers inform us, it was bodily pain: "a violent headache, saith Tertullian; (*De Pudic*) to which both Chrysostom and St. Jerome agree. St. Cyprian [*De Mortalitate*] expresses it, a little more generally, in those terms: "Many and grievous torments of the flesh and of the body." [*Carnis et corporis multa ac gravia tormenta*] Thirdly, to this exactly agree the Apostle's own words, "A thorn to the flesh to smite, beat, or buffet me." "My strength is made perfect in weakness:" — Which same word occurs no less than four times in these two verses only. But, Fourthly, whatsoever it was, it could not be either inward or outward sin. It could no more be inward stirrings, than outward expressions, of pride, anger, or lust. This is manifest, beyond all possible exception from the words that immediately follow: "Most gladly will I glory in" these "my weaknesses, that the strength of Christ may rest upon me." [2 Cor. 12:9] What! Did he glory in pride, in anger, in lust? Was it through these *weaknesses*, that the strength of Christ rested upon him? He goes on: "Therefore I take pleasure in weaknesses; for when I am weak, then am I strong;" [2 Cor. 12:10] that is, when I am weak *in body*, then am I strong *in spirit*. But will any man dare to say, "When I am weak by pride or

lust, then am I strong in spirit?" I call you all to record this day, who find the strength of Christ resting upon you, can you glory in anger, or pride, or lust? Can you take pleasure in these infirmities? Do these weaknesses make you strong? Would you not leap into hell, were it possible, to escape them? Even by yourselves, then, judge, whether the Apostle could glory and take pleasure in them! Let it be, Lastly, observed, that this thorn was given to St. Paul above fourteen years before he wrote this Epistle; [2 Cor. 12:2] which itself was wrote several years before he finished his course. [See Acts 20:24; 2 Tim. 4:7] So that he had after this, a long course to run, many battles to fight, many victories to gain, and great increase to receive in all the gifts of God, and the knowledge of Jesus Christ. Therefore from any spiritual weakness (if such it had been) which he at that time felt, we could by no means infer that he was never made strong; that Paul the aged, the father in Christ, still laboured under the same weaknesses; that he was in no higher state till the day of his death. From all which it appears that this instance of St. Paul is quite foreign to the question, and does in no wise clash with the assertion of St. John, "He that is born of God sinneth not." [1 John 5:18]

17. "But does not St. James directly contradict this? His words are, 'In many things we offend all,' (Jas. 3:2) And is not offending the same as committing sin?" In this place, I allow it is: I allow the persons here spoken of did commit sin; yea, that they all committed many sins. But who are the persons here spoken of? Why, those many masters or teachers whom God had not sent; (probably the same vain men who taught that faith without works, which is

so sharply reproved in the preceding chapter;) [Jas. 2] not the Apostle himself, nor any real Christian. That in the word *we* (used by a figure of speech common in all other, as well as the inspired, writings) the Apostle could not possibly include himself or any other true believer, appears evidently, First, from the same word in the ninth verse: — "Therewith," saith he, "bless we God and therewith curse we men. Out of the same mouth proceedeth blessing and cursing." [Jas. 3:9] True; but not out of the mouth of the Apostle, nor of anyone who is in Christ a new creature. [2 Cor. 5:17] Secondly, from the verse immediately preceding the text, and manifestly connected with it: "My brethren, be not many masters," (or teachers,) "knowing that we shall receive the greater condemnation." "For in many things we offend all." [Jas. 3:1] *We!* Who? Not the Apostles, not true believers; but they who know they should *receive the greater condemnation*, because of those many offences. But this could not be spoke of the Apostle himself, or of any who trod in his steps, seeing "there is no condemnation to them who walk not after the flesh, but after the Spirit." [Rom. 8:2] Nay, Thirdly, the very verse itself proves, that "we offend all," cannot be spoken either of all men, or of all Christians: For in it there immediately follows the mention of a man who *offends not*, as the *we* first mentioned did; from whom, therefore, he is professedly contradistinguished, and pronounced a *perfect man*.

18. So clearly does St. James explain himself, and fix the meaning of his own words. Yet, lest any one should still remain in doubt, St. John, writing many years after St. James, puts the matter entirely out of dispute, by the express declarations above recited. But here a fresh

difficulty may arise: How shall we reconcile St. John with himself? In one place he declares, "Whosoever is born of God doth not commit sin;" [1 John 3:9] and again, — "We know that he which is born of God sinneth not:" [1 John 5:18] And yet in another he saith, "If we say that we have no sin, we deceive ourselves, and the truth is not in us;" [1 John 1:8] and again, — "If we say that we have not sinned, we make him a liar, and his word is not in us." [1 John 1:10]

19. As great a difficulty as this may at first appear, it vanishes away, if we observe, First, that the tenth verse fixes the sense of the eighth: "If we say we have no sin," in the former, being explained by, "If we say we have not sinned," in the latter verse. [1 John 1:10, 8] Secondly, that the point under present consideration is not whether we *have or have not sinned heretofore*; and neither of these verses asserts that we *do sin, or commit sin now*. Thirdly, that the ninth verse explains both the eighth and tenth. "If we confess our sins, he is faithful and just to forgive us our sins, and to cleanse us from all unrighteousness:" As if he had said, "I have before affirmed, 'The blood of Jesus Christ cleanseth us from all sin;' but let no man say, I need it not; I have no sin to be cleansed from. If we say that we have no sin, that we have not sinned, we deceive ourselves, and make God a liar: But if we confess our sins, he is faithful and just, not only 'to forgive our sins,' but also 'to cleanse us from all unrighteousness:' [1 John 1:8-10] that we may 'go and sin no more.' " [John 8:11]

20. St. John, therefore, is well consistent with himself, as well as with the other holy writers; as will yet more evidently appear if we place all his assertions touching this matter in one view: He declares, First, the blood of Jesus Christ

cleanseth us from all sin. Secondly, no man can say, I have not sinned, I have no sin to be cleansed from. Thirdly, but God is ready both to forgive our past sins and to save us from them for the time to come. [1 John 1:7-10] Fourthly, "These things I write unto you," saith the Apostle, "that ye may not sin. But if any man" should "sin," or *have sinned,* (as the word might be rendered,) he need not continue in sin; seeing "we have an Advocate with the Father, Jesus Christ the righteous." [1 John 2:1-2] Thus far all is clear. But lest any doubt should remain in a point of so vast importance, the Apostle resumes this subject in the third chapter, and largely explains his own meaning. "Little children," saith he, "let no man deceive you:" (As though I had given any encouragement to those that continue in sin:) "He that doeth righteousness is righteous, even as He is righteous. He that committeth sin is of the devil; for the devil sinneth from the beginning. For this purpose the Son of God was manifested, that he might destroy the works of the devil. Whosoever is born of God doth not commit sin: For his seed remaineth in him; and he cannot sin, because he is born of God. In this the children of God are manifest, and the children of the devil." (1 John 3:7-10) Here the point, which till then might possibly have admitted of some doubt in weak minds, is purposely settled by the last of the inspired writers, and decided in the clearest manner. In conformity, therefore, both to the doctrine of St. John, and to the whole tenor of the New Testament, we fix this conclusion — *A Christian is so far perfect, as not to commit sin.*

21. This is the glorious privilege of every Christian; yea, though he be but *a babe in Christ.* But it is only of those

who *are strong* in the Lord, and "have overcome the wicked one," or rather of those who "have known him that is from the beginning," [1 John 2:13, 14] that it can be affirmed they are in such a sense perfect, as, Secondly, to be freed from evil thoughts and evil tempers. First, from evil or sinful thoughts. But here let it be observed, that thoughts concerning evil are not always evil thoughts; that a thought concerning sin, and a sinful thought, are widely different. A man, for instance, may think of a murder which another has committed; and yet this is no evil or sinful thought. So our blessed Lord himself doubtless thought of, or understood the thing spoken by the devil, when he said, "All these things will I give thee, if thou wilt fall down and worship me." [Matt. 4:9] Yet had he no evil or sinful thought; nor indeed was capable of having any. And even hence it follows, that neither have real Christians: for "every one that is perfect is as his Master." (Luke 6:40) Therefore, if He was free from evil or sinful thoughts, so are they likewise.

22. And, indeed, whence should evil thoughts proceed, in the servant who is *as his Master?* "Out of the heart of man" (if at all) "proceed evil thoughts." (Mark 7:21) If, therefore, his heart be no longer evil, then evil thoughts can no longer proceed out of it. If the tree were corrupt, so would be the fruit: But the tree is good; The fruit, therefore is good also; (Matt. 22:33) our Lord himself bearing witness, "Every good tree bringeth forth good fruit. A good tree cannot bring forth evil fruit," as "a corrupt tree cannot bring forth good fruit." (Matt 7:17, 18)

23. The same happy privilege of real Christians, St. Paul asserts from his own experience. "The weapons of our

warfare," saith he, "are not carnal, but mighty through God to the pulling down of strongholds; casting down imaginations" (or *reasonings* rather, for so the word *logimous* signifies; all the reasonings of pride and unbelief against the declarations, promises, or gifts of God) "and every high thing that exalteth itself against the knowledge of God, and bringing into captivity every thought to the obedience of Christ." (2 Cor. 10:4, &c.)

24. And as Christians indeed are freed from evil thoughts, so are they, Secondly, from evil tempers. This is evident from the above-mentioned declaration of our Lord himself: "The disciple is not above his Master; but every one that is perfect shall be as his Master." [Luke 6:40] He had been delivering, just before, some of the sublimest doctrines of Christianity, and some of the most grievous to flesh and blood. "I say unto you, love your enemies, do good to them which hate you; — and unto him that smiteth thee on the one cheek, offer also the other." [Luke 6:29] Now these he well knew the world would not receive; and, therefore, immediately adds, "Can the blind lead the blind? Will they not both fall into the ditch?" [Luke 6:39] As if he had said, "Do not confer with flesh and blood touching these things, — with men void of spiritual discernment, the eyes of whose understanding God hath not opened, — lest they and you perish together." In the next verse he removes the two grand objections with which these wise fools meet us at every turn: "These things are too grievous to be borne," or, "They are too high to be attained," [Matt. 23:4] saying, " 'The disciple is not above his Master;' therefore, if I have suffered, be content to tread in my steps. And doubt ye not then, but I will fulfill my word: 'For every one that

is perfect shall be as his Master.' " [Luke 6:40] But his Master was free from all sinful tempers. So, therefore, is his disciple, even every real Christian.

25. Every one of these can say, with St. Paul, "I am crucified with Christ: Nevertheless I live; yet not I, but Christ liveth in me:" [Gal 2:20] — Words that manifestly describe a deliverance from inward as well as from outward sin. This is expressed both negatively, *I live not;* (my evil nature, the body of sin, is destroyed;) and positively, *Christ liveth in me;* and, therefore, all that is holy, and just, and good. Indeed, both these, *Christ liveth in me,* and *I live not,* are inseparably connected; for "what communion hath light with darkness, or Christ with Belial?" [2 Cor. 6:15]

26. He, therefore, who liveth in true believers, hath "purified their hearts by faith;" [Acts 15:9] insomuch that every one that hath Christ in him the hope of glory, [Col. 1:27] "purifieth himself, even as he is pure" (1 John 3:3) He is purified from pride; for Christ was lowly of heart. [Matt. 11:29] He is pure from self-will or desire; for Christ desired only to do the will of his Father, and to finish his work. [John 4:34; 5:30] And he is pure from anger, in the common sense of the word; for Christ was meek and gentle, patient and long-suffering. I say, in the common sense of the word; for all anger is not evil. We read of our Lord himself, (Mark 3:5) that he once "looked round with anger." But with what kind of anger? The next word shows, *sullupoumenos,* being, at the same time "grieved for the hardness of their hearts." [Mark 3:6] So then he was angry at the sin, and in the same moment grieved for the sinners; angry or displeased at the offence, but sorry for the offenders. With anger, yea, hatred, he looked upon the thing; with grief and love upon

the persons. Go, thou that art perfect, and do likewise. Be thus angry, and thou sinnest not; [see Eph. 4:26] feeling a displacency at every offence against God, but only love and tender compassion to the offender.

27. Thus doth Jesus "save his people from their sins:" [Matt. 1:21] And not only from outward sins, but also from the sins of their hearts; from evil thoughts and from evil tempers. — "True," say some, "we shall thus be saved from our sins; but not till death; not in this world." But how are we to reconcile this with the express words of St. John? — "Herein is our love made perfect, that we may have boldness in the day of judgment. Because as he is, so are we in this world." The Apostle here, beyond all contradiction, speaks of himself and other living Christians, of whom (as though he had foreseen this very evasion, and set himself to overturn it from the foundation) he flatly affirms, that not only at or after death but *in this world* they are as their Master. (1 John 4:17)

28. Exactly agreeable to this are his words in the first chapter of this Epistle, (1 John 1:5, &c.) "God is light, and in him is no darkness at all. If we walk in the light, — we have fellowship one with another, and the blood of Jesus Christ his Son cleanseth us from all sin." And again, "If we confess our sins, he is faithful and just to forgive us our sins, and to cleanse us from all unrighteousness." [1 John 1:9] Now it is evident, the Apostle here also speaks of a deliverance wrought *in this world.* For he saith not, the blood of Christ will cleanse at the hour of death, or in the day of judgment, but, it "cleanseth," at the time present, "us," living Christians, "from all sin." And it is equally evident, that if *any sin* remain, we are not cleansed from *all sin*: If

any unrighteousness remain in the soul, it is not cleansed from *all* unrighteousness. Neither let any sinner against his own soul say, that this relates to justification only, or the cleansing us from the guilt of sin. First, because this is confounding together what the Apostle clearly distinguishes, who mentions first, *to forgive us our sins,* and then *to cleanse us from all unrighteousness.* "Secondly, because this is asserting justification by works, in the strongest sense possible; it is making all inward as well as outward holiness necessarily previous to justification. For if the cleansing here spoken of is no other than the cleansing us from the guilt of sin, then we are not cleansed from guilt; that is, are not justified, unless on condition of "walking in the light, as he is in the light." [1 John 1:7] It remains, then, that Christians are saved in this world from all sin, from all unrighteousness; that they are now in such a sense perfect, as not to commit sin, and to be freed from evil thoughts and evil tempers."

29. Thus hath the Lord fulfilled the things he spake by his holy prophets, which have been since the world began; — by Moses in particular, saying, (Deut. 30:6) I "will circumcise thine heart, and the heart of thy seed, to love the Lord thy God with all thy heart, and with all thy soul;" by David, crying out, "Create in me a clean heart, and renew a right spirit within me;" [Ps. 51:10] — and most remarkably by Ezekiel, in those words: "Then will I sprinkle clean water upon you, and ye shall be clean; From all your filthiness, and from all your idols, will I cleanse you. A new heart also will I give you, and a new spirit will I put within you; — and cause you to walk in my statutes, and ye shall keep my judgments, and do them. — Ye shall be my people,

and I will be your God. I will also save you from all your uncleannesses. — Thus saith the Lord your God, In the day that I shall have cleansed you from all your iniquities, — the Heathen shall know that I the Lord build the ruined places; — I the Lord have spoken it, and I will do it." (Ezek. 36:25, &c.)

30. "Having therefore these promises, dearly beloved," both in the Law and in the Prophets, and having the prophetic word confirmed unto us in the Gospel, by our blessed Lord and his Apostles; "let us cleanse ourselves from all filthiness of flesh and spirit, perfecting holiness in the fear of God." [2 Cor. 7:1] "Let us fear, lest" so many "promises being made us of entering into his rest," which he that hath entered into, has ceased from his own works, "any of us should come short of it." [Heb. 4:1] "This one thing let us do, forgetting those things which are behind, and reaching forth unto those things which are before, let us press toward the mark, for the prize of the high calling of God in Christ Jesus;" [Phil. 3:13, 14] crying unto him day and night, till we also are "delivered from the bondage of corruption, into the glorious liberty of the sons of God!" [Rom. 8:21]

Appendix 2: "The Promise of Sanctification"

(Ezekiel 36:25, &c.)
BY THE REV. CHARLES WESLEY

This is written in an unusual meter, but it can easily be sung to the tune of "Amazing Grace" if you hold the last note in the second and fourth lines to fit the extra words. Spelling and punctuation are Wesley's.

God of all power, and truth, and grace,
   Which shall from age to age endure;
   Whose word, when heaven and earth shall pass,
   Remains, and stands for ever sure:

Calmly to thee my soul looks up,
   And waits thy promises to prove;
   The object of my steadfast hope,
   The seal of thine eternal love.

That I thy mercy may proclaim,
   That all mankind thy truth may see,
   Hallow thy great and glorious name,
   And perfect holiness in me.

Chose from the world, if now I stand
   Adorn'd in righteousness divine;
   If, brought unto the promised land,
   I justly call the Saviour mine;

Perform the work thou hast begun,
   My inmost soul to thee convert:
   Love me, for ever love thine own,
   And sprinkle with thy blood my heart.

Thy sanctifying Spirit pour,
   To quench my thirst, and wash me clean;
   Now, Father, let the gracious shower
   Descend, and make me pure from sin.

Purge me from every sinful blot;
   My idols all be cast aside:
   Cleanse me from every evil thought,
   From all the filth of self and pride.

Give me a new, a perfect heart,
   From doubt, and fear, and sorrow free;
   The mind which was in Christ impart,
   And let my spirit cleave to thee.

O take this heart of stone away,

(Thy rule it doth not, cannot own;)
In me no longer let it stay:
O take away this heart of stone.

The hatred of my carnal mind
Out of my flesh at once remove;
Give me a tender heart, resign'd,
And pure, and fill'd with faith and love.

Within me thy good Spirit place,
Spirit of health, and love and power;
Plant in me thy victorious grace,
And sin shall never enter more.

Cause me to walk in Christ my Way,
And I thy statutes shall fulfill;
In every point thy law obey.
And perfectly perform thy will.

Hast thou not said, who canst not lie,
That I thy law shall keep and do?
Lord, I believe, though men deny;
They all are false, but thou art true.

O that I now, from sin released,
Thy word might to the utmost prove!
Enter into the promised rest,
The Canaan of thy perfect love!

There let me ever, ever dwell;
By thou my God, and I will be

Thy servant: O set to thy seal!
Give me eternal life in thee.

From all remaining filth within
Let me in Thee salvation have:
From actual, and from inbred sin
My ransom'd soul persist to save.

Wash out my old original stain:
Tell me no more, "It cannot be,"
Demons or men! The Lamb was slain
His blood was all poured out for me!

Sprinkle it, Jesu, on my heart:
One drop of thy all-cleansing blood
Shall make my sinfulness depart,
And fill me with the life of God.

Father, supply my every need:
Sustain the life thyself hast given;
Call for the corn, the living bread,
The manna that comes down from heaven.

The gracious fruits of righteousness,
Thy blessings' unexhausted store,
In me abundantly increase;
Nor let me ever hunger more.

Let me no more in deep complaint
"My leanness, O my leanness!" cry;
Alone consumed with pining want,

Of all my Father's children I!

The painful thirst, the fond desire,
    Thy joyous presence shall remove;
    While my full soul doth still require
    Thy whole eternity of love.

Holy, and true, and righteous Lord,
    I wait to prove thy perfect will;
    Be mindful of thy gracious word,
    And stamp me with thy Spirit's seal!

Thy faithful mercies let me find,
    In which thou causest me to trust;
    Give me the meek and lowly mind,
    And lay my spirit in the dust.

Show me how foul my heart hath been,
    When all renew'd by grace I am:
    When thou hast emptied me of sin,
    Show me the fulness of my shame.

Open my faith's interior eye,
    Display thy glory from above;
    And all I am shall sink and die,
    Lost in astonishment and love.

Confound, o'erpower me with thy grace:
    I would be by myself abhorr'd;
    (All might, all majesty, all praise,
    All glory be to Christ my Lord!)

Now let me gain perfection's height!
   Now let me into nothing fall!
   Be less than nothing in thy sight,
   And feel that Christ is all in all!

Notes

INTRODUCTION

1   "Preface to the Sermons," from *The Works of John Wesley*, Third American Edition

2   Wording updated

3   *If any of you is lacking in wisdom, ask God, who gives to all generously and ungrudgingly, and it will be given you.* (James 1:5)

4   *Thus says the Lord, your Redeemer, the Holy One of Israel: I am the Lord your God, who teaches you for your own good, who leads you in the way you should go.* (Isaiah 48:17)

5   *These things we also speak, not in words which man's wisdom teaches but which the Holy Spirit teaches, comparing spiritual things with spiritual.* (1 Corinthians 2:13 NKJV)

6   *This book of the law shall not depart out of your mouth; you shall meditate on it day and night, so that you may be careful to act in accordance with all that is written in it. For then you shall make your way prosperous, and then you shall be successful."* (Joshua 1:8)

7   *Now the promises were made to Abraham and to his offspring; it does not say, "And to offsprings," as of many; but it says, "And to your offspring," that is, to one person, who is Christ.* (Galatians 3:16)

"CHRISTIAN PERFECTION," BY JOHN WESLEY

8   From Philippians 3:12 (KJV); NRSV reads, *Not that I have already obtained this or have already reached the goal.*

9   *Therefore I declare to you this day that I am not responsible for the blood of any of you, for I did not shrink from declaring to you the whole purpose of God.* (Acts 20:26–27)

10   *I press on toward the goal for the prize of the heavenly call of God in Christ Jesus.* (Philippians 3:14)

11   From Philippians 3:12 (KJV). NRSV reads, *Not that I have already obtained this or have already reached the goal.*

12   From Philippians 3:15 (KJV). NRSV reads, *Let those of us then who are mature be of the same mind.*

13   *Those who are unspiritual do not receive the gifts of God's Spirit, for they are foolishness to them, and they are unable to understand them because they are spiritually discerned.* (1 Corinthians 2:14)

14   *See what love the Father has given us, that we should be called children of God; and that is what we are. The reason the world does not know us is that it did not know him.* (1 John 3:1)

15   *I pray that, according to the riches of his glory, he may grant that you may be strengthened in your inner being with power through his Spirit, and that Christ may dwell in your hearts through faith, as you are being rooted and grounded in love.* (Ephesians 3:16–17)

16   *Trust in the Lord with all your heart, And lean not on your own understanding; In all your ways acknowledge Him, And He shall direct your paths.* (Proverbs 3:5–6 NKJV)

17   *We know that all things work together for good for those who love God, who are called according to his purpose.* (Romans 8:28)

18   *He has told you, O mortal, what is good; and what does the Lord require of you but to do justice, and to love kindness, and to walk humbly with your God?* (Micah 6:8)

19   *Therefore I do my best always to have a clear conscience toward God and all people.* (Acts 24:16)

20   *These are indeed but the outskirts of his ways; and how small a whisper do we hear of him! But the thunder of his power who can understand?"* (Job 26:14)

21   *For there are three that bear witness in heaven: the Father, the Word, and the Holy Spirit; and these three are one.* (1 John 5:7 NKJV)

22   *But emptied himself, taking the form of a slave, being born in human likeness. And being found in human form, he humbled himself and became obedient to the point of death— even death on a cross.* (Philippians 2:7–8)

23   *And He said to them, "It is not for you to know times or seasons which the Father has put in His own authority.* (Acts 1:7 NKJV)

24   *Surely the Lord God does nothing, without revealing his secret to his servants the prophets.* (Amos 3:7)

25   *But the day of the Lord will come like a thief, and then the heavens will pass away with a loud noise, and the elements will be dissolved with fire, and the earth and everything that is done on it will be disclosed.* (2 Peter 3:10)

26   *Clouds and thick darkness are all around him; righteousness and justice are the foundation of his throne.* (Psalm 97:2)

27   *Jesus answered, "You do not know now what I am doing, but later you will understand."* (John 13:7)

28   *He stretches out the north over empty space; He hangs the earth on nothing.* (Job 26:7 NKJV)

29   *For now we see in a mirror, dimly, but then we will see face to face. Now I know only in part; then I will know fully, even as I have been fully known.* (1 Corinthians 13:12)

30   *Ah, you who call evil good and good evil, who put darkness for light and light for darkness, who put bitter for sweet and sweet for bitter!* (Isaiah 5:20)

31   *Do not invite death by the error of your life, or bring on destruction by the works of your hands.* (Wisdom of Solomon 1:12) Wisdom of Solomon is one of the apocryphal or deuterocanonical books included in some Bibles. They are usually considered inspired in the sense that we might say the writings of a favorite devotional author or theologian are inspired, but without the divine authority of the canonical or standard accepted books of the Bible.

32   *As for you, the anointing that you received from him abides in you, and so you do not need anyone to teach you. But as his anointing teaches you about all things, and is true and is not a lie, and just as it has taught you, abide in him.* (1 John 2:27)

33   *A highway shall be there, and it shall be called the Holy Way; the unclean shall not travel on it, but it shall be for God's people; no traveler, not even fools, shall go astray.* (Isaiah 35:8)

34   *But you have an anointing from the Holy One, and you know all things.* 1 John 2:20 (NKJV) "You" is plural both times in this verse.

35   *Beloved, I pray that all may go well with you and that you may be in good health, just as it is well with your soul.* (3 John 2)

36   *"But about that day and hour no one knows, neither the angels of heaven, nor the Son, but only the Father.* (Matthew 24:36)

37   *I write these things to you concerning those who would deceive you.* (1 John 2:26)

38 *Let no one deceive you with empty words, for because of these things the wrath of God comes on those who are disobedient.* (Ephesians 5:6); see also Mark 13:5; 2 Thessalonians 2:3

39 *But I say to you that if you are angry with a brother or sister, you will be liable to judgment; and if you insult a brother or sister, you will be liable to the council; and if you say, 'You fool,' you will be liable to the hell of fire.* (Matthew 5:22)

40 *Do not repay evil for evil or abuse for abuse; but, on the contrary, repay with a blessing. It is for this that you were called—that you might inherit a blessing.* (1 Peter 3:9)

41 Wesley is not suggesting that those he describes are less valuable or loved in God's sight. He is referring to the perspective of a world that judges people according to what we today would call standardized tests.

42 *Then the dust will return to the earth as it was, and the spirit will return to God who gave it.* (Ecclesiastes 12:7 NKJV)

43 *They have lost all sensitivity and have abandoned themselves to licentiousness, greedy to practice every kind of impurity.* (Ephesians 4:19)

44 *Holding to the outward form of godliness but denying its power. Avoid them!* (2 Timothy 3:5)

45 *Therefore, since we are justified by faith, we have peace with God through our Lord Jesus Christ,* (Romans 5:1)

46 *In him we have redemption through his blood, the forgiveness of our trespasses, according to the riches of his grace.* (Ephesians 1:7)

47 *Saying, "Do not touch my anointed ones; do my prophets no harm."* (1 Chronicles 16:22)

48 *He made him ride in the heights of the earth, That he might eat the produce of the fields; He made him draw honey from the rock, And oil from the flinty rock.* (Deuteronomy 32:13 NKJV)

49 *You have seen what I did to the Egyptians, and how I bore you on eagles' wings and brought you to myself.* (Exodus 19:4)

50 *With all of these, take the shield of faith, with which you will be able to quench all the flaming arrows of the evil one.* (Ephesians 6:16)

51 *For we do not have a High Priest who cannot sympathize with our weaknesses, but was in all points tempted as we are, yet without sin.* (Hebrews 4:15 NKJV)

52 *A disciple is not above the teacher, but everyone who is fully qualified will be like the teacher.* (Luke 6:40)

REAL CHRISTIANS DON'T SIN

53 *But grow in the grace and knowledge of our Lord and Savior Jesus Christ. To him be the glory both now and to the day of eternity. Amen.* (2 Peter 3:18)

54 *And this is my prayer, that your love may overflow more and more with knowledge and full insight* (Philippians 1:9)

55 *I am writing to you, little children, because your sins are forgiven on account of his name.* (1 John 2:12)

56 *Therefore, since we are justified by faith, we have peace with God through our Lord Jesus Christ,* (Romans 5:1)

57 *I am writing to you, young people, because you have conquered the evil one . . . I write to you, young people, because you are strong and the word of God abides in you, and you have overcome the evil one.* (1 John 2:13–14)

58 *With all of these, take the shield of faith, with which you will be able to quench all the flaming arrows of the evil one.* (Ephesians 6:16)

59 *I write to you, fathers, because you have known Him who is from the beginning. I write to you, young men, because you have overcome the wicked one. I write to you, little children, because you have known the Father.* (1 John 2:13 NKJV)

60 *Till we all come to the unity of the faith and of the knowledge of the Son of God, to a perfect man, to the measure of the stature of the fullness of Christ;* (Ephesians 4:13 NKJV)

61 *Certainly not! Indeed, let God be true but every man a liar. As it is written: "That You may be justified in Your words, And may overcome when You are judged."* (Romans 3:4 NKJV)

62 Wesley defines justification as "another word for pardon. It is the forgiveness of all our sins; and, what is necessarily implied therein, our acceptance with God." (John Wesley, Sermon 43, "The Scripture Way of Salvation.")

63 *What then are we to say? Should we continue in sin in order that grace may abound? By no means! How can we who died to sin go on living in it?* (Romans 6:1–2)

64 *For if we have been united with him in a death like his, we will certainly be united with him in a resurrection like his.* (Romans 6:5)

65 *We know that our old self was crucified with him so that the body of sin might be destroyed, and we might no longer be enslaved to sin.* (Romans 6:6)

66 *For whoever has died is freed from sin.* (Romans 6:7)

67   *The death he died, he died to sin, once for all; but the life he lives, he lives to God. So you also must consider yourselves dead to sin and alive to God in Christ Jesus.* (Romans 6:10–11)

68   *For sin will have no dominion over you, since you are not under law but under grace.* (Romans 6:14)

69   *And that you, having been set free from sin, have become slaves of righteousness.* (Romans 6:18)

70   *Since therefore Christ suffered in the flesh, arm yourselves also with the same intention (for whoever has suffered in the flesh has finished with sin), so as to live for the rest of your earthly life no longer by human desires but by the will of God.* (1 Peter 4:1–2)

71   *Everyone who commits sin is a child of the devil; for the devil has been sinning from the beginning. The Son of God was revealed for this purpose, to destroy the works of the devil. Those who have been born of God do not sin, because God's seed abides in them; they cannot sin, because they have been born of God.* (1 John 3:8–9)

72   *We know that those who are born of God do not sin, but the one who was born of God protects them, and the evil one does not touch them.* (1 John 5:18)

"BUT DOESN'T THE OLD TESTAMENT SAY...?"

73   *Now there was a famine in the land. So Abram went down to Egypt to reside there as an alien, for the famine was severe in the land. When he was about to enter Egypt, he said to his wife Sarai, "I know well that you are a woman beautiful in appearance; and when the Egyptians see you, they will say, 'This is his wife'; then they will kill me, but they will let you live. Say you are my sister, so that it may go well with me because of you, and that my life may be spared on your account."* (Genesis 12:10–13)

74   *The Lord spoke to Moses, saying: "Take the staff, and assemble the congregation, you and your brother Aaron, and command the rock before their eyes to yield its water."* . . . *Then Moses lifted up his hand and struck the rock* . . . *But the Lord said to Moses and Aaron, "Because you did not trust in me, to show my holiness before the eyes of the Israelites, therefore you shall not bring this assembly into the land that I have given them."* (Numbers 20:7–12)

Moses' sin was that God had commanded him to speak to the rock but instead he hit it with his stick. Striking a rock in this way can sometimes naturally release water trapped behind a thin crust of stone. This allowed doubters to claim it was not a miracle, just natural forces at work.

75   *And when He had removed him, He raised up for them David as king, to whom also He gave testimony and said, 'I have found David the son of Jesse, a man after My own heart, who will do all My will.'* (Acts 13:22 NKJV)

76   David committed adultery with Uriah's wife Bathsheba, then had Uriah killed to cover it up (2 Samuel 11).

77   *Truly I tell you, among those born of women no one has arisen greater than John the Baptist; yet the least in the kingdom of heaven is greater than he.* (Matthew 11:11)

78   *From the days of John the Baptist until now the kingdom of heaven has suffered violence, and the violent take it by force.* (Matthew 11:12)

79   *I tell you, among those born of women no one is greater than John; yet the least in the kingdom of God is greater than he.* (Luke 7:28)

80   "Dispensation" is a theological term referring to the way God works with humans in different times. Scholars divide dispensations up in different ways, but the most basic is the time before the law was given to Moses, the time between Moses and Jesus, and the time after Jesus' time on earth.

81   *But if the ministry of death, written and engraved on stones, was glorious, so that the children of Israel could not look steadily at the face of Moses because of the glory of his countenance, which glory was passing away, how will the ministry of the Spirit not be more glorious? For if the ministry of condemnation had glory, the ministry of righteousness exceeds much more in glory.* (2 Corinthians 3:7–9 NKJV)

82   *As many of you as were baptized into Christ have clothed yourselves with Christ.* (Galatians 3:27)

83   *Jesus answered them, "You are wrong, because you know neither the scriptures nor the power of God."* (Matthew 22:29)

84   *For a righteous man may fall seven times and rise again, but the wicked shall fall by calamity.* (Proverbs 24:16 NKJV)

85   *Do not lie in wait like an outlaw against the home of the righteous; do no violence to the place where the righteous live.* (Proverbs 24:15)

86   *For though they fall seven times, they will rise again; but the wicked are overthrown by calamity.* (Proverbs 24:16)

87   *If they sin against you—for there is no one who does not sin—and you are angry with them and give them to an enemy, so that they are carried away captive to the land of the enemy, far off or near;* (1 Kings 8:46)

88   *Surely there is no one on earth so righteous as to do good without ever sinning.* (Ecclesiastes 7:20)

89   *My point is this: heirs, as long as they are minors, are no better than slaves, though they are the owners of all the property.* (Galatians 4:1)

90   *So with us; while we were minors, we were enslaved to the elemental spirits of the world. But when the fullness of time had come, God sent his Son, born of a woman, born under the law, in order to redeem those who were under the law, so that we might receive adoption as children.* (Galatians 4:3–5)

91   *But it has now been revealed through the appearing of our Savior Christ Jesus, who abolished death and brought life and immortality to light through the gospel.* (2 Timothy 1:10)

92   *So you are no longer a slave but a child, and if a child then also an heir, through God.* (Galatians 4:7)

93   *We know that those who are born of God do not sin, but the one who was born of God protects them, and the evil one does not touch them.* (1 John 5:18)

94   *"And let the one who believes in me drink. As the scripture has said, 'Out of the believer's heart shall flow rivers of living water.' " Now he said this about the Spirit, which believers in him were to receive; for as yet there was no Spirit, because Jesus was not yet glorified.* (John 7:38–39)

95   *Cure the sick, raise the dead, cleanse the lepers, cast out demons. You received without payment; give without payment.* (Matthew 10:8)

96   *Therefore it is said, "When he ascended on high he made captivity itself a captive; he gave gifts to his people."* (Ephesians 4:8)

97   *You have ascended on high, you have led captivity captive; you have received gifts among men, even from the rebellious, that the Lord God might dwell there.* (Psalm 68:18 NKJV)

98   *When the day of Pentecost had come, they were all together in one place. And suddenly from heaven there came a sound like the rush of a violent wind, and it filled the entire house where they were sitting. Divided tongues, as of fire, appeared among them, and a tongue rested on each of them. All of them were filled with the Holy Spirit and began to speak in other languages, as the Spirit gave them ability.* (Acts 2:1–4)

99   *While staying with them, he ordered them not to leave Jerusalem, but to wait there for the promise of the Father. "This," he said, "is what you have heard from me."* (Acts 1:4)

100 *No, in all these things we are more than conquerors through him who loved us.* (Romans 8:37)

101 *For you are receiving the outcome of your faith, the salvation of your souls. Concerning this salvation, the prophets who prophesied of the grace that was to be yours made careful search and inquiry, inquiring about the person or time that the Spirit of Christ within them indicated when it testified in advance to the sufferings destined for Christ and the subsequent glory. It was revealed to them that they were serving not themselves but you, in regard to the things that have now been announced to you through those who brought you good news by the Holy Spirit sent from heaven—things into which angels long to look!* (1 Peter 1:9–12)

102 *Therefore prepare your minds for action; discipline yourselves; set all your hope on the grace that Jesus Christ will bring you when he is revealed. Like obedient children, do not be conformed to the desires that you formerly had in ignorance. Instead, as he who called you is holy, be holy yourselves in all your conduct; for it is written, "You shall be holy, for I am holy."* (1 Peter 1:13–16)

103 *But when the fullness of time had come, God sent his Son, born of a woman, born under the law.* (Galatians 4:4)

104 *He has rescued us from the power of darkness and transferred us into the kingdom of his beloved Son.* (Colossians 1:13)

105 *On that day the Lord will shield the inhabitants of Jerusalem so that the feeblest among them on that day shall be like David, and the house of David shall be like God, like the angel of the Lord, at their head.* (Zechariah 12:8)

106 *We know that those who are born of God do not sin, but the one who was born of God protects them, and the evil one does not touch them.* (1 John 5:18)

107 *So I do not run aimlessly, nor do I box as though beating the air.* (1 Corinthians 9:26)

"BUT DOESN'T THE NEW TESTAMENT SAY...?"

108 *The disagreement became so sharp that they parted company; Barnabas took Mark with him and sailed away to Cyprus.* (Acts 15:39)

109 *For until certain people came from James, he used to eat with the Gentiles. But after they came, he drew back and kept himself separate for fear of the circumcision faction. And the other Jews joined him in this hypocrisy, so that even Barnabas was led astray by their hypocrisy.* (Galatians 2:12–13)

110 *No temptation has overtaken you except such as is common to man; but God is faithful, who will not allow you to be tempted beyond what you are able, but*

91

with the temptation will also make the way of escape, that you may be able to bear it. (1 Corinthians 10:13 NKJV)

111 *Three times I appealed to the Lord about this, that it would leave me,* (2 Corinthians 12:8)

112 *Even considering the exceptional character of the revelations. Therefore, to keep me from being too elated, a thorn was given me in the flesh, a messenger of Satan to torment me, to keep me from being too elated. Three times I appealed to the Lord about this, that it would leave me, but he said to me, "My grace is sufficient for you, for power is made perfect in weakness." So, I will boast all the more gladly of my weaknesses, so that the power of Christ may dwell in me. Therefore I am content with weaknesses, insults, hardships, persecutions, and calamities for the sake of Christ; for whenever I am weak, then I am strong.* (2 Corinthians 12:7–10)

113 2 Corinthians 12:7 (see note 112)

114 2 Corinthians 12:9 (see note 112)

115 2 Corinthians 12:9 (see note 112)

116 *Therefore I take pleasure in infirmities, in reproaches, in needs, in persecutions, in distresses, for Christ's sake. For when I am weak, then I am strong.* (2 Corinthians 12:10 NKJV)

117 *I know a person in Christ who fourteen years ago was caught up to the third heaven—whether in the body or out of the body I do not know; God knows.* (2 Corinthians 12:2)

118 *I have fought the good fight, I have finished the race, I have kept the faith.* (2 Timothy 4:7)

119 *We know that those who are born of God do not sin, but the one who was born of God protects them, and the evil one does not touch them.* (1 John 5:18)

120 *For all of us make many mistakes. Anyone who makes no mistakes in speaking is perfect, able to keep the whole body in check with a bridle.* (James 3:2)
    The King James Version, which Wesley used, reads "offend" for "make mistakes."

121 *With it we bless the Lord and Father, and with it we curse those who are made in the likeness of God. From the same mouth come blessing and cursing. My brothers and sisters, this ought not to be so.* (James 3:9–10)

122 *So if anyone is in Christ, there is a new creation: everything old has passed away; see, everything has become new!* (2 Corinthians 5:17)

123 *My brethren, let not many of you become teachers, knowing that we shall receive a stricter judgment. For we all stumble in many things. If anyone does not stumble in word, he is a perfect man, able also to bridle the whole body.* (James 3:1–2 NKJV) The King James Version, which Wesley used, reads "greater condemnation" for "stricter judgment," and "offend" for "stumble."

124 *There is therefore now no condemnation to those who are in Christ Jesus, who do not walk according to the flesh, but according to the Spirit.* (Romans 8:1 NKJV)

125 *For all of us make many mistakes. Anyone who makes no mistakes in speaking is perfect, able to keep the whole body in check with a bridle.* (James 3:2)

126 *Those who have been born of God do not sin, because God's seed abides in them; they cannot sin, because they have been born of God.* (1 John 3:9)

127 *We know that those who are born of God do not sin, but the one who was born of God protects them, and the evil one does not touch them.* (1 John 5:18)

128 *If we say that we have no sin, we deceive ourselves, and the truth is not in us.* (1 John 1:8)

129 *If we say that we have not sinned, we make him a liar, and his word is not in us.* (1 John 1:10)

130 *If we confess our sins, he who is faithful and just will forgive us our sins and cleanse us from all unrighteousness.* (1 John 1:9)

131 *She said, "No one, Lord." And Jesus said to her, "Neither do I condemn you; go and sin no more."* (John 8:11 NKJV)

132 *But if we walk in the light as he himself is in the light, we have fellowship with one another, and the blood of Jesus his Son cleanses us from all sin.* (1 John 1:7)

133 *If we say that we have no sin, we deceive ourselves, and the truth is not in us.* (1 John 1:8)

134 *If we confess our sins, he who is faithful and just will forgive us our sins and cleanse us from all unrighteousness.* (1 John 1:9)

135 *My little children, I am writing these things to you so that you may not sin. But if anyone does sin, we have an advocate with the Father, Jesus Christ the righteous; and he is the atoning sacrifice for our sins, and not for ours only but also for the sins of the whole world.* (1 John 2:1–2)

136 *Little children, let no one deceive you. Everyone who does what is right is righteous, just as he is righteous. Everyone who commits sin is a child of the devil; for the devil has been sinning from the beginning. The Son of God was*

revealed for this purpose, to destroy the works of the devil. Those who have been born of God do not sin, because God's seed abides in them; they cannot sin, because they have been born of God. The children of God and the children of the devil are revealed in this way: all who do not do what is right are not from God, nor are those who do not love their brothers and sisters. (1 John 3:7–10)

137 *And so, brothers and sisters, I could not speak to you as spiritual people, but rather as people of the flesh, as infants in Christ.* (1 Corinthians 3:1)

FREE INSIDE

138 *I am writing to you, fathers, because you know him who is from the beginning. I am writing to you, young people, because you have conquered the evil one.* (1 John 2:13)

139 *And he said to him, "All these I will give you, if you will fall down and worship me."* (Matthew 4:9)

140 *A disciple is not above the teacher, but everyone who is fully qualified will be like the teacher.* (Luke 6:40)

141 *For it is from within, from the human heart, that evil intentions come: fornication, theft, murder,* (Mark 7:21)

142 *In the same way, every good tree bears good fruit, but the bad tree bears bad fruit. A good tree cannot bear bad fruit, nor can a bad tree bear good fruit.* (Matthew 7:17–18)

143 *For the weapons of our warfare are not merely human, but they have divine power to destroy strongholds. We destroy arguments and every proud obstacle raised up against the knowledge of God, and we take every thought captive to obey Christ.* (2 Corinthians 10:4–5)

144 *A disciple is not above the teacher, but everyone who is fully qualified will be like the teacher.* (Luke 6:40)

145 *But I say to you that listen, Love your enemies, do good to those who hate you, bless those who curse you, pray for those who abuse you. If anyone strikes you on the cheek, offer the other also; and from anyone who takes away your coat do not withhold even your shirt. Give to everyone who begs from you; and if anyone takes away your goods, do not ask for them again.* (Luke 6:27–30)

146 *He also told them a parable: "Can a blind person guide a blind person? Will not both fall into a pit?"* (Luke 6:39)

147 *Those who are unspiritual do not receive the gifts of God's Spirit, for they are foolishness to them, and they are unable to understand them because they are spiritually discerned.* (1 Corinthians 2:14)

148 *A disciple is not above the teacher, but everyone who is fully qualified will be like the teacher.* (Luke 6:40)

149 *For through the law I died to the law, so that I might live to God. I have been crucified with Christ; and it is no longer I who live, but it is Christ who lives in me. And the life I now live in the flesh I live by faith in the Son of God, who loved me and gave himself for me.* (Galatians 2:19–20)

150 *What agreement does Christ have with Beliar? Or what does a believer share with an unbeliever?* (2 Corinthians 6:15) "Beliar," often spelled "Belial," was another name for Satan.

151 *And in cleansing their hearts by faith he has made no distinction between them and us.* (Acts 15:9)

152 *To them God chose to make known how great among the Gentiles are the riches of the glory of this mystery, which is Christ in you, the hope of glory.* (Colossians 1:27)

153 *And all who have this hope in him purify themselves, just as he is pure.* (1 John 3:3)

154 *Take my yoke upon you, and learn from me; for I am gentle and humble in heart, and you will find rest for your souls.* (Matthew 11:29)

155 *Jesus said to them, "My food is to do the will of him who sent me and to complete his work."* (John 4:34)

156 *I myself, Paul, appeal to you by the meekness and gentleness of Christ—I who am humble when face to face with you, but bold toward you when I am away!* (2 Corinthians 10:1)

157 *He looked around at them with anger; he was grieved at their hardness of heart and said to the man, "Stretch out your hand." He stretched it out, and his hand was restored.* (Mark 3:5)

158 *He said, "The one who showed him mercy." Jesus said to him, "Go and do likewise."* (Luke 10:37)

159 *Be angry but do not sin; do not let the sun go down on your anger, and do not make room for the devil.* (Ephesians 4:26–27)

160 *She will bear a son, and you are to name him Jesus, for he will save his people from their sins.* (Matthew 1:21)

161 *Love has been perfected among us in this: that we may have boldness on the day of judgment, because as he is, so are we in this world.* (1 John 4:17)

162 *This is the message we have heard from him and proclaim to you, that God is light and in him there is no darkness at all. If we say that we have fellowship*

with him while we are walking in darkness, we lie and do not do what is true; but if we walk in the light as he himself is in the light, we have fellowship with one another, and the blood of Jesus his Son cleanses us from all sin. (1 John 1:5–7)

163 *If we confess our sins, he who is faithful and just will forgive us our sins and cleanse us from all unrighteousness.* (1 John 1:9)

164 *But if we walk in the light as he himself is in the light, we have fellowship with one another, and the blood of Jesus his Son cleanses us from all sin.* (1 John 1:7)

165 Justification is the status of being set right with God through confession and forgiveness, with the result that we are cleansed of guilt in a legal sense. Wesley's argument is that the passage says God not only cleanses us from the guilt of our sins, but also from the unrighteousness that leads us to commit sins.

166 *If we confess our sins, he who is faithful and just will forgive us our sins and cleanse us from all unrighteousness.* (1 John 1:9)

167 Justification by works is the idea that we must earn forgiveness and salvation by how we live or the works we do. This is the opposite of the Biblical teaching that we receive forgiveness and salvation by faith as a gift of God's grace. *For by grace you have been saved through faith, and this is not your own doing; it is the gift of God— not the result of works, so that no one may boast.* (Ephesians 2:8–9)

168 *But if we walk in the light as he himself is in the light, we have fellowship with one another, and the blood of Jesus his Son cleanses us from all sin.* (1 John 1:7)

169 *Moreover, the Lord your God will circumcise your heart and the heart of your descendants, so that you will love the Lord your God with all your heart and with all your soul, in order that you may live.* (Deuteronomy 30:6)

170 *Create in me a clean heart, O God, and put a new and right spirit within me.* (Psalm 51:10)

171 Selected portions from Ezekiel chapter 36, verses 25, 26, 27, 33, and 36

172 In common theological short-hand, "the Law and the Prophets" refers to the Old Testament and "the Gospel" to the New Testament.

173 *Since we have these promises, beloved, let us cleanse ourselves from every defilement of body and of spirit, making holiness perfect in the fear of God.* (2 Corinthians 7:1)

174 *For those who enter God's rest also cease from their labors as God did from his.* (Hebrews 4:10)

175 *Therefore, while the promise of entering his rest is still open, let us take care that none of you should seem to have failed to reach it.* (Hebrews 4:1)

176 *Beloved, I do not consider that I have made it my own; but this one thing I do: forgetting what lies behind and straining forward to what lies ahead, I press on toward the goal for the prize of the heavenly call of God in Christ Jesus.* (Philippians 3:13–14)

177 *That the creation itself will be set free from its bondage to decay and will obtain the freedom of the glory of the children of God.* (Romans 8:21)

178 *For through the law I died to the law, so that I might live to God. I have been crucified with Christ; and it is no longer I who live, but it is Christ who lives in me. And the life I now live in the flesh I live by faith in the Son of God, who loved me and gave himself for me.* (Galatians 2:19–20)

About the Author

Best known internationally as author of PASTORING: THE NUTS AND BOLTS, in print in seven languages, David Wentz has a passion for helping people connect with God and make a difference. Combining 38 years as a pastor with a first career in engineering and graduate degrees from three very different seminaries (charismatic, mainstream, and Wesleyan-evangelical), he expresses God's truth in ways everyone can appreciate.

Raised in the Episcopal church, Dr. Wentz has also been part of Nazarene, Pentecostal Holiness, and non-denominational congregations. As a Methodist pastor he served small, large, and multicultural churches in rural, small-town, suburban, and urban settings, served as a regional church consultant in the Maryland – D.C. area, and led workshops for pastors internationally. In 2015 he retired to the rural Ozarks, where he writes, works in God's great outdoors, and oversees Doing

Christianity, Inc., a small non-profit devoted to equipping pastors in developing and minority-Christian countries.

In 1974, David married his college sweetheart, Paula. They have five children with wonderful spouses, and fourteen grandchildren.

The book of Ezekiel describes David's calling. Twenty-five hundred years ago God called Ezekiel to teach God's ways and proclaim the Holy Spirit, who revives dry bones and forms them into a dwelling for God and a source of living water that heals nations.

Bones are still dry today. God still wants to dwell among his people. Nations still need healing. And people still need to be taught God's ways and be moved by God's Spirit. That's what David calls "Doing Christianity."

You can connect with me on:

🌐 https://www.pastordavidwentz.com

📘 https://www.facebook.com/profile.php?id=100064901162331

Subscribe to my newsletter:

✉️ https://mailchi.mp/c162e27f817b/doing-christianity-email-newsletter-sign-up

Also by David Wentz

Christianity is about more than just going to heaven when you die. It's about becoming like Jesus and living the Kingdom of God in this life. That not only blesses us, it blesses everyone around. That's what I call doing Christianity, and it's what my books are all about.

John Wesley's "The Character of a Methodist:" Set in Modern Language with Introduction and Suggestions for Group Use
A perennial best-seller since its publication, this summary of the root emphases of Wesley's teaching is required reading in today's turbulent times. Father of Methodism and grandfather of Pentecostalism and the Salvation Army, Wesley shows the character of a true Christian of any denomination. Part of the John Wesley in Modern Language series.

John Wesley's "The New Birth:" Set in Modern Language with Introduction and Suggestions for Group Use

Is being good the way to heaven? Being religious? Jesus said, "You must be born again. John Wesley explains Jesus' words in this brief classic. One of the standard sermons Wesley required his circuit riders to learn and re-preach, *The New Birth* shows that religion and morality are good but new life in Jesus is vital. Part of the John Wesley in Modern Language series.

When Church Stops Working: Meeting With God in Your Living Room

If you ever led a meeting or taught a class, you and your friends can be a fully functioning part of God's work in the world.

For pastors, here's a proven way to extend your reach by mentoring living-room church leaders and networks.

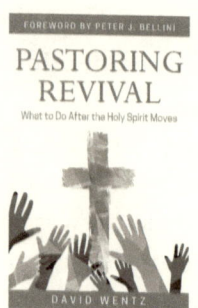

Pastoring Revival: What to Do After the Holy Spirit Moves

"Come, Holy Spirit!" Then what? Few pastors are trained what to do if God answers with unusual power. Drawing on two fascinating case studies, academic research, and his own thirty-eight years as a pastor, seeker, and student of revival, Dr. Wentz has produced a practical, engaging, Biblical, actionable guide to prepare every pastor for the next great move of God.

"It's hard to put to words how excited this book makes me. I have pastored for years . . . Read this book, and get ready." — Amazon reviewer

Pastoring: The Nuts and Bolts — Options and Best Practices for Leading a Church

Crossing denominations and cultures and solidly grounded in Scripture, *Pastoring* offers options and best practices instead of dogmatic assertions. It moves from God's purpose for the church to the pastor's personal life, then covers worship, preaching, leadership, administration, and issues relevant to charismatic and Pentecostal churches not normally addressed in this kind of book. In seven languages and counting, *Pastoring* has blessed thousands of new and seasoned pastors.